THE WINDOW
IN TWENTIETH-CENTURY ART

Organized by
Suzanne Delehanty

NEUBERGER MUSEUM

State University of New York at Purchase

Front Cover:
HENRI MATISSE
The Green Pumpkin circa 1920
Museum of Art, Rhode Island School of Design
Anonymous gift

LIBRARY OF CONGRESS
CATALOGING-IN-PUBLICATION DATA

Delehanty, Suzanne, 1944–
    The window in twentieth-century art.

    Exhibition held at Neuberger Museum, Purchase, N.Y. 21 September 1986 to 18 January 1987 and at Contemporary Arts Museum, Houston, Tex. 24 April 1987 to 29 June 1987.
    Bibliography: p. 104.
    Contents: The open window / Shirley Neilsen Blum—The artist's window / Suzanne Delehanty.
    1. Windows in art—Exhibitions.
    2. Art, Modern—20th century—Exhibitions. I. Blum, Shirley Neilsen. II. Neuberger Museum. III. Contemporary Arts Museum. IV. Title.
N8261.W56D45   1986
709'.04'00740147277   86-61058
ISBN 0-934032-08-4

SOURCES OF QUOTATIONS
Guillaume Apollinaire, "Windows," *Selected Writings of Guillaume Apollinaire,* trans. Roger Shattuck (London: The Harvill Press, 1950), pp. 141–43.

Charles Baudelaire, "Windows," *Paris Spleen*, trans. Louise Varèse (New York: A New Directions Book, 1947), p. 77.

Stéphane Mallarmé, "The Windows," trans. Hubert Creekmore, *Stéphane Mallarmé: Selected Poetry and Prose,* ed. Mary Ann Caws (New York: A New Directions Book, 1982), p. 11.

Rainer Maria Rilke. "Windows III," *The Roses and the Windows,* trans. A. Poulin, Jr. (Port Townsend, WA: Gray Wolf Press, 1979), p. 75.

Designed by Drenttel Doyle Partners
Typeset by Trufont Typographers
Production Consultant:
Michael Josefowicz

Type: Mergenthaler Garamond #3
Papers: Warren LOE Dull, 100# Text, Champion Kromekote 12 pt. Cover, Curtis Tweedweave 80# Text

Three thousand copies published by
Neuberger Museum
State University of New York
at Purchase
September 1986

Back Cover:
MARCEL DUCHAMP
Fresh Widow 1920 (third version 1964)
Indiana University Art Museum
Partial gift of Mrs. William Conroy

TABLE OF CONTENTS   THE WINDOW IN TWENTIETH-CENTURY ART

THE WINDOW IN TWENTIETH-CENTURY ART

Neuberger Museum
State University of New York
at Purchase
Purchase, New York

21 SEPTEMBER 1986 TO 18 JANUARY 1987

Contemporary Arts Museum
Houston, Texas

24 APRIL 1987 TO 29 JUNE 1987

★

Major funding for this exhibition and publication was provided by: the National Endowment for the Arts, a federal agency; the Westchester Arts Fund of the Council for the Arts in Westchester, supported by corporate contributions and the County of Westchester; Neuberger & Berman; the Roy R. and Marie S. Neuberger Foundation; and the Philip H. and Lois R. Steckler Foundation.

SIAH ARMAJANI
RICHARD ARTSCHWAGER
MILTON AVERY
BALTHUS
ROBERT BERLIND
MARC CHAGALL
CHRISTO
JOSEPH CORNELL
GENE DAVIS
ROBERT DELAUNAY
RICHARD DIEBENKORN
MARCEL DUCHAMP
RAOUL DUFY
DON EDDY
RICHARD ESTES
JANE FREILICHER
ADOLPH GOTTLIEB
JUAN GRIS
MARSDEN HARTLEY
EVA HESSE
DAVID HOCKNEY
HOWARD HODGKIN
HANS HOFMANN
EDWARD HOPPER
RALPH HUMPHREY
BRYAN HUNT
NEIL JENNEY
JASPER JOHNS
ELLSWORTH KELLY
EDWARD KIENHOLZ AND
NANCY REDDIN KIENHOLZ
SHIGEKO KUBOTA
ROY LICHTENSTEIN
RENE MAGRITTE
SYLVIA PLIMACK MANGOLD
HENRI MATISSE
ROBERT MOSKOWITZ
ROBERT MOTHERWELL
CATHERINE MURPHY
PETE OMLOR
PABLO PICASSO
FAIRFIELD PORTER
MARK ROTHKO
GEORGE SEGAL
MARK TANSEY
EDOUARD VUILLARD
JOHN WALKER
TOM WESSELMANN
WILLIAM T. WILEY

ACKNOWLEDGMENTS

The notion of presenting an exhibition on the window in art of our century has been simmering at the Museum for several years. Although the window in art is an age-old and oft discussed topic, this is the first exhibition in the United States to explore the subject. The survey, which we hope will stimulate additional study of this broad and intriguing theme, focuses primarily on the window in American art and includes a number of works from the Museum's own holdings. The selection concentrates on works by artists who have drawn upon the theme of the window over a sustained period of time or have investigated the motif with great intensity at a particular moment in their development. A group of works by the early European modernists also is presented to provide a historical framework for the theme, which has sparked the invention of generations of younger European artists as well.

The realization of the exhibition owes a great deal to the skill and enthusiastic cooperation of a good number of persons. On behalf of the Neuberger Museum, I would like to extend our gratitude to all of them. I would especially like to acknowledge the early assistance of Ella Schaap, who undertook the preliminary research for the project. Carla Gottlieb, whose extensive publications on the window are a major contribution to the field, kindly met with me when the thought of such an exhibition was at its inception. We extend our appreciation to the following individuals for their generosity in sharing information with us through conversation or correspondence: Richard Ader; Schellie Hagan; Lynda Roscoe Hartigan, National Museum of American Art, Smithsonian Institution; Sidney Janis; Ellen Johnson, Allen Memorial Art Museum at Oberlin College; Neil Printz, Rice University; Mark Rosenthal, Philadelphia Museum of Art; Cora Rosevear, The Museum of Modern Art, New York; William Rubin, The Museum of Modern Art, New York; and Charles F. Stuckey, National Gallery of Art, Washington, DC. We would like to offer our special thanks also to Leo Castelli and Susan Brundage of the Leo Castelli Gallery, Nathan Kolodner of the André Emmerich Gallery, Betty Cunningham of Hirschl & Adler Modern, and Renato Danese and Susan Sturges at The Pace Gallery for help well beyond the common measure. At Purchase, James Boyles, Visual Arts Librarian, provided his expert assistance in securing research materials with ever-ready cheerfulness.

My warmest appreciation to the Museum's entire staff for their special efforts in bringing the exhibition and publication to completion. I would particularly like to single out Sigrid Goldiner, whose contribution to the project far exceeded that of Research Assistant. Collaborator would be more apt! She gathered research material and compiled the bibliography and managed all the correspondence and documents for the exhibition with undaunting vigor and thoroughness. Additionally, she served as coordinator of the publication, which benefited from her meticulous sense of detail and unflappable understanding of production schedules. Above all, she contributed a critical and thoughtful eye and mind as well as a generous spirit, for which I am most deeply indebted. Michael Reed, Special Project Consultant, brought to the exhibition his impressive organizational abilities and a refined understanding of the requirements of packing, handling, and installing works of art; we are also truly grateful to him for his calmness and absolute reliability. Olga D'Angelo, Curatorial Assistant, prepared all the correspondence related to the project as well as the manuscripts for publication with great precision, dependability, and good-hearted kindness. Nancy Miller, Assistant Director, and Douglas Caulk, Museum Manager, assumed many of my administrative responsibilities in the last stages of the exhibition's realization; I extend my thanks to them for their exceptional support. Along with these added responsibilities, Nancy Miller kindly read my essay and provided many valuable suggestions, and Douglas Caulk has overseen the installation with great sensitivity and intelligence. Administrative Assistant Claire Powers kept everyone on schedule with a singular sense of humor.

The publication for the exhibition represents the creativity of many persons. We are extremely grateful to Shirley Neilsen Blum, Professor of the History of Art, State University of New York at Purchase, for a lively and insightful essay from the perspective of a Renaissance scholar with a keen appreciation and knowledge of the art of the twentieth century. I am grateful also for the pleasure of our conversations throughout the year; they have greatly enriched the project. We would like to acknowledge Sarah Williams of W2 for her prepublication editorial advice. Constance Stallings served as editor for the publication, which reflects her unerring sense of accuracy; we extend our warm thanks for her good-natured flexibility. The catalogue was designed by Tom Kluepfel of Drenttel Doyle Partners; our enthusiastic thanks to him for his sympathetic and inventive design and to Katy Delehanty for assisting with the design and coordination of the publication. Sylvia Quesada, Summer Intern at the design firm, also contributed to the catalogue's realization. Michael Josefowicz of Red Ink expertly handled production.

Exhibitions are ultimately the result of the generosity of lenders. On behalf of the Neuberger Museum, I would like to offer my most sincere appreciation to the individuals and institutions listed for parting with much treasured works of art for the presentation of the exhibition at Purchase and in Houston. The exhibition would not have been possible without their extraordinary cooperation.

Exhibitions and publications begin as ideas and dreams. We are exceedingly grateful to the National Endowment for the Arts, a federal agency; Neuberger & Berman; the Roy R. and Marie S. Neuberger Foundation; and Philip H. and Lois R. Steckler Foundation for generous support of the project. We are indebted also to the Westchester Arts Fund of the Council for the Arts in Westchester, which is supported by corporate contributions and the County of Westchester, for grants for both planning and publication.

It is a great privilege to present *The Window in Twentieth-Century Art* to the Museum's academic and regional publics. We are pleased that the exhibition will be actively integrated into the study of art, literature, and film as well as the other disciplines in the interdisciplinary curriculum at Purchase. We also appreciate Linda L. Cathcart's early enthusiasm for the exhibition's theme and are delighted that the exhibition will travel, under her direction, to the Contemporary Arts Museum in Houston.

Suzanne Delehanty, Director
Neuberger Museum
State University of New York
at Purchase

LENDERS TO THE EXHIBITION

Robert E. Abrams Family Collection, New York

Akron Art Museum, Akron, Ohio

Albright–Knox Art Gallery, Buffalo, New York

Charles Altschul

André Emmerich Gallery, New York

The Art Institute of Chicago, Chicago

Mrs. Robert M. Benjamin, New York

Robert Berlind, New York

The Edward R. Broida Trust, Los Angeles

Mr. and Mrs. Leo Castelli, New York

Leo Castelli Gallery, New York

The Chase Manhattan Bank, N.A.

Cincinnati Art Museum, Cincinnati, Ohio

Columbus Museum of Art, Columbus, Ohio

Estate of Joseph Cornell

Mrs. Robert B. Eichholz

Mr. and Mrs. I. Irving Feldman

Shirley and Miles Fiterman, Minneapolis

Mr. and Mrs. Victor W. Ganz

Sondra G. Gilman

Adolph and Esther Gottlieb Foundation, Inc., New York

Agnes Gund, New York

Mr. and Mrs. James Harithas, Houston, Texas

Mrs. Wellington Henderson, California

Hirshhorn Museum and Sculpture Garden, Smithsonian Institution, Washington, DC

Indiana University Art Museum, Bloomington, Indiana

Mr. and Mrs. William C. Janss

Neil Jenney, New York

Jasper Johns, New York

Ellsworth Kelly

Shigeko Kubota, New York

Lannan Foundation

Lippincott Foundry, North Haven, Connecticut

L.A. Louver Gallery, Venice, California

McNay Art Museum, San Antonio, Texas

The Morgan Gallery, Kansas City, Kansas

Robert Moskowitz, New York

Robert Motherwell, Connecticut

Museum of Art, Rhode Island School of Design, Providence, Rhode Island

Museum of Contemporary Art, Chicago

The Museum of Modern Art, New York

National Gallery of Art, Washington, DC

Roy R. Neuberger, New York

Neuberger Museum, State University of New York at Purchase, Purchase, New York

Oklahoma Art Center, Oklahoma City, Oklahoma

Oliver–Hoffmann Collection

The Parrish Art Museum, Southampton, New York

The Phillips Collection, Washington, DC

Mr. and Mrs. Joseph Pulitzer, Jr., Saint Louis, Missouri

Dr. and Mrs. Raymond Sackler

The Saint Louis Art Museum, Saint Louis, Missouri

Martin Sklar, New York

Smith College Museum of Art, Northampton, Massachusetts

Holly and Horace Solomon, New York

Stedelijk Museum, Amsterdam

Virginia Museum of Fine Arts, Richmond, Virginia

Warner Communications Inc., New York

Whitney Museum of American Art, New York

William T. Wiley, California

Williams College Museum of Art, Williamstown, Massachusetts

Six Private Collectors

Above:
CATHERINE MURPHY
Nighttime Self-Portrait 1985
Collection Mrs. Robert M. Benjamin

I flee and cling to all the window frames
Whence one can turn his back on life in scorn,
And, blest, in their glass, by eternal dewdrops laved
And gilded by the Infinite's chaste morn,

I peer and see myself an angel! I die, I long
—Let the window be art, be mystic state—
To be reborn, wearing my dream as a crown,
In the previous heaven where Beauty flowered great!

STÉPHANE MALLARMÉ
"The Windows" 1863

THE OPEN WINDOW : A RENAISSANCE VIEW

Let me tell you what I do when I am painting. First of all, on the surface on which I am going to paint, I draw a rectangle of whatever size I want, which I regard as an open window through which the subject to be painted is seen.

LEON BATTISTA ALBERTI

WITH THESE TEXTBOOK instructions,[1] Leon Battista Alberti codified, in 1435, a practice which, by the end of the fifteenth century, had become familiar to nearly every Florentine artist. The relation of a picture to a view seen through a window has been associated ever since with the development of Renaissance art. For the first time since the Classical era, the art of painting became self-consciously the art of imitation. The painter's increasing desire to create the appearance of three-dimensionality on a two-dimensional surface led rapidly to a systematic descrip-

tion of space and to the discovery of focal-point perspective. The use of Alberti's imaginary window linked the history of the window with the history of perspective.[2] The window frame provided the necessary limits for the internal perspectival plan. The transversals and orthogonals of the geometric system of perspective formed a grid that began and ended at the framing edge. As if receding behind the surface of the window, all the objects laid out upon this grid could be represented in proportion to each other and to the space they occupied as they gradually diminished toward the horizon line.

Illus. 1. From ALBRECHT DÜRER, *The Painter's Manual*, 1525, ed. Walter L. Strauss, Abaris Books, New York, 1977

by Shirley Neilsen Blum

The new painting presented a monocular view of space best seen by the spectator when he was positioned in the exact place initially determined by the artist. Perspective governed not only the external position of the viewer, but all the internal elements of the painting. The all-controlling focal point determined the viewer's optimal distance from the work and the level of his eye. If the spectator did not maintain this position, his view was imperfect.

Though perspective statically fixes the spectator and the scene he beholds, it also unites them. Whether single- or multi-point, perspective suggests that the view through the window is an extension of the natural world. Even a sacred event is brought to life within a space and setting empirically identified with that of the viewer. Alberti tells us

that such means of representation, forgotten during the Middle Ages, appeared almost miraculous to the Renaissance viewer: "Painting possesses a truly divine power in that not only does it make the absent present (as they say of friendship), but it also represents the dead to the living."[3]

An illustration by Albrecht Dürer for his treatise on perspective (illus. 1), composed almost a hundred years after Alberti, demonstrates this theory. The vertex of the cone of vision, the artist's eye, is fixed by the use of a sight. As Alberti describes it, a net or grill is placed between the artist and the object to be represented, intersecting the cone of vision at right angles. The artist duplicates this grid on his canvas or panel and locates on it a series of points, in proper relative position, based upon his observation of the subject through the grill. In his print Dürer dramatized the advantage of the method by selecting an overtly voluptuous female for his subject. With the help of perspective, he captured the emphatic mass of the woman on a two-dimensional surface.

Focal-point perspective, which was primarily an art of arithmetically measured space, exerted a new control over the world of representation. Within its confines, man and his buildings and God and His landscape shared a single, scientifically apportioned space. Divinities were no longer represented much larger than humans; their

9

size, like all else within the picture, usually depended only upon their relative position in space, not upon their superior nature.

Fra Angelico's *Annunciation* (illus. 2), commissioned about 1438 for the monastery of San Marco in Florence, exemplifies the new Renaissance invention. Here the worldly and the divine meet within a setting put in somewhat imperfect mathematical order by perspective. The moment of Incarnation takes place beneath an arcade that imitates that of the actual cloister, which was designed at virtually the same time by the architect Michelozzo. In both painting and reality the architecture is graceful and pure. In the Fra Angelico fresco the classical restraint of the arcade enhances the gentle, sweet nature of the humble Virgin and the attentive Archangel. The sanctity of the setting is established by the inherent purity of the geometric order, made apparent through the use of perspective and clear spatial volumes, and by classical associations attached to the architectural forms themselves. Rather than diminishing the scene by topicality, the artist's use of contemporary architecture further enshrines the figures within a familiar and sacred space.

To Alberti, as to many Renaissance thinkers, God's presence could be expressed through perfect geometric forms. He wrote, for example, that the ideal church should be in the form of a circle. The assertion of geometrically derived proportions, the use of balanced forms, and the rhythmic repetition of regular units were seen as imitations of a sacred order. Such configurations evoked the divine by association with power of pure reason, just as the laws that govern the movement of the planets were equated with those found in mathematical relations and musical harmonies. Perspective was a tool well suited to this Neoplatonic thinking. It could formalize spatial projections and hence was capable of raising naturalistic description to an ideal realm.

From Early Christian times the body of the Virgin, because it held Christ, was often linked to a receptacle. To remind the devout of Mary's role as protective, virginal vessel she was metaphorically called a tabernacle, a sealed chamber, or a closed window. In the Angelico *Annunciation* the focal point rests upon a tiny, barred window, or *fenestra cancellata*, a rectangle symbolic, as is the closed cell and the enclosed garden, of the virginity of Mary. An even greater number of Mary's saintly attributes were associated with an open window. Because an open window looks

out onto another world, Christ and the Virgin were frequently represented behind a parapet, as if they were looking through a window from the divine realm into our world. As man's foremost advocate before God, the Mother of Christ could intercede for man and thereby provide him an entry into Paradise. In this role she was represented by a variety of architectural forms: door or gate as well as window. As the *fenestra caeli* she symbolized the window of heaven through which shone the divine light of the Savior.

Although most Southern Renaissance paintings embody the notion of a window view in the use of perspective, very few windows were actually depicted. It was in the Netherlands that the window flourished as a pictorial and symbolic device. *The Mérode Altarpiece* (illus. 3), painted

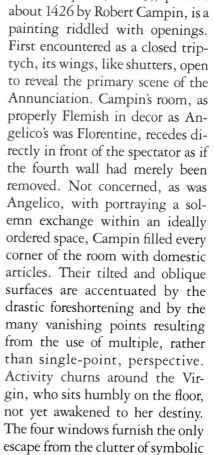

Top:
Illus. 2. FRA ANGELICO, *The Annunciation*, circa 1438, fresco, 90 × 125 inches (228.6 × 317.5 cms). Museo San Marco, Florence

Bottom:
Illus. 3. ROBERT CAMPIN, *The Mérode Altarpiece*, circa 1426, oil on wood, central panel: 25¼ × 24⅞ inches (64.1 × 63.2 cms), each wing: 25⅜ × 10¾ inches (64.5 × 27.3 cms). The Metropolitan Museum of Art, purchase, The Cloisters Collection

about 1426 by Robert Campin, is a painting riddled with openings. First encountered as a closed triptych, its wings, like shutters, open to reveal the primary scene of the Annunciation. Campin's room, as properly Flemish in decor as Angelico's was Florentine, recedes directly in front of the spectator as if the fourth wall had merely been removed. Not concerned, as was Angelico, with portraying a solemn exchange within an ideally ordered space, Campin filled every corner of the room with domestic articles. Their tilted and oblique surfaces are accentuated by the drastic foreshortening and by the many vanishing points resulting from the use of multiple, rather than single-point, perspective. Activity churns around the Virgin, who sits humbly on the floor, not yet awakened to her destiny. The four windows furnish the only escape from the clutter of symbolic objects which seem to press their foreshortened edges hard against the pictorial surface.

Only the pure light and air of the heavens enters this sacred room. The double window behind the Virgin opens to the blue sky. The two circular windows are closed and further fortified by lead mullions which contrast with the transparency of the glass and the purity of the light. Seven rays of light, symbolic of the seven rays of wisdom, stream through the sacred circle. The tiny Christ Child slides down one of these beams to meet his human fate. This manner of godly Incarnation, so delicately portrayed by Campin, directly parallels medieval texts. One text, a hymn to the Nativity, chants a verbal equivalent: "As a sunbeam through the glass Passeth but not breaketh, So the Virgin, as she was, Virgin still remaineth."[4]

Equating light with divinity is as old as man himself.

10

Many Early Christian texts drew analogies between Christ and the sun. Both are a fundamental source of life: one provides the spiritual, the other the physical light of the world. The Emperor Constantine further legitimized the union between Christ and the sun by precociously embedding Christian attributes in symbolism and liturgy previously reserved for the sun god. During the later Romanesque period, light came to be a metaphor, also, for the two miraculous births: that of Mary in the Immaculate Conception and Christ in the Incarnation. Campin's altarpiece glistens with the symbolic light of the Incarnation. Closed circular windows, penetrating rays, and tiny homunculus all announce the wondrous birth.

On the right wing of *The Mérode Altarpiece*, Joseph the carpenter sits in a rectangular, brown workshop, which contrasts with the square, white, upper room of Mary. Joseph's room is viewed diagonally so as to enhance the centrality of the Annunciation setting. Rather than being a heavenly window in a secular chapel, the window of Joseph's shop opens out from a lower floor upon a bustling Flemish city. Joseph is of this world. Born of man, he can never attain the sacred heights of the Virgin and Christ. His betrothal to the Virgin, according to Saint Augustine, was intended to fool the devil into believing that Christ was fathered by a mortal and hence could not be divine. Saint Augustine called Joseph the bait in the *muscipula diaboli*,[5] the devil's mousetrap. As painted by Campin, the mousetrap is a large Flemish contraption prominently displayed in the window of Joseph's shop. Its presence within Campin's wide array of symbols joins Joseph's paternal role to his profession as carpenter.

Illus. 4. JAN VAN EYCK, *The Virgin in the Church*, circa 1427, oil on wood, 12 × 5½ inches (30.5 × 14 cms). Staatliche Museen, Preussischer Kulturbesitz, Gemäldegalerie, Berlin

Many worldly objects, such as the mousetrap or the window, were associated in the medieval mind with particular religious concepts. Because these equivalencies have often gone unrecognized by the contemporary viewer, Erwin Panofsky called them "disguised symbols." The symbolism attached to the window illustrates the precarious balance between the worldly appearance and the otherworldly meaning so characteristic of sacred painting in the Renaissance. The painter's consuming desire to replicate the thousands of forms newly discovered in nature was steadily held in check by the demands of the work's religious subject and function. The challenge lay in portraying the sacred event as if it were at once of man's time and forever beyond it. None understood better the power of this apparent contradiction than the artists of the Netherlands.

Jan van Eyck's small painting of *The Virgin in the Church* from about 1427 (illus. 4) contains symbolic light so subtle as to appear almost magical in both form and meaning. An enormous Virgin, now visually identified with the entire church structure as *Maria ecclesia*, stands in the center of the nave. Her crown, delicately modeled in harmony with the sculpted decoration of the rood screen behind her, reaches almost to the level of the clerestory; her heavily robed body stretches transversely from the aisle colonnade to the center of the church. Light floods in through the windows above her head, empirically impossible in any correctly oriented Gothic church, for the light to her right should be coming from the dim north side. Instead it shines with the brightness of a southern exposure. This can be no ordinary edifice: a lofty Virgin fills the nave, angels say mass at the altar, and the sun has changed its course. The intricate Gothic structure and the heroic Woman each symbolize the establishment of God's church on earth. The two natures of Christ, human babe and Almighty God, are expressed by the two spots of supernatural light that fall mystically upon the floor in the center of the nave.

The molded wooden frame that surrounds van Eyck's picture was painted to simulate marble. Renaissance frames in both the north and south of Europe often imitated heavy architectural constructions, as this one does. When the pictorial image more closely mirrored nature, the frame assumed greater importance. It located the definitive boundary between the pictorial and the real world. But, like perspective, the frame also united fable and fact. While asserting a concrete boundary for the pictorial fiction, the frame could extend the pictorial experience directly into living space as, for example, when it served as the actual casement of a window through which we look at a given scene. The frame could simulate stone inscribed with verses which enlarged the narrative of the painting, and it often furnished a convenient shelf on which to rest a painted book or hand.

In Petrus Christus' severe *Portrait of a Carthusian* of 1446 (illus. 5), the frame provides a permanent sill for a fictive, wandering fly. Although probably a warning of the mortality of flesh, this trompe l'oeil effect remains unexplained. Were it a butterfly hovering about a vase of flowers painted some two hundred years later, we would not view it with such surprise, for in the sixteenth and seven- 11 teenth centuries a painted window frame served as a fine resting-place for many a bit of still or animal life. In this much earlier work, however, the barrier of the frame seems nearly dissolved by the dialogue between the holy monk, who looks out sharply, and the viewer, who cannot take his eyes off the lowly fly.

One of the most remarkable series of window spaces from the Renaissance is found in the diptych of the *Virgin and Child with Portrait of Martin van Nieuwenhove* (illus. 6) painted by Hans Memling in 1487. The donor occupies the right wing in three-quarter profile and looks toward the Virgin, who is presented frontally. Although painted on separate panels, the two figures are located illusionistically in the corner of one room—she against the back wall, he against an oblique wall. The bull's-eye mirror behind the Virgin reveals that they are positioned next to each other behind a continuous loggia which separates them from the space of the viewer. The ledge conforms to the lower frame of the painting, and the separating column seen in the mirror has been replaced or disguised by the break between the two panels. The unity of the space, which permits the donor to occupy the same room as the Virgin and Child, is reenforced by the continuous landscape seen through all the windows. Only the actual frame of the diptych and the implied column separate the donor from the Virgin, both physically and symbolically. In every other illusionistic sense he shares her space or, more exactly, she his. For the interior is decidedly Flemish and associated with Nieuwenhove; his coat of arms and Saint Martin, his patron saint, appear in the stained glass.

Illus. 5. PETRUS CHRISTUS, *Portrait of a Carthusian*, 1446, tempera and oil, 11½ × 8 inches (29.2 × 20.3 cms). The Metropolitan Museum of Art, The Jules Bache Collection

The viewer is captivated by the conceit of three separate window spaces. In the first, the actual frame of the diptych encloses the double portrait of donor and Virgin. This double view gives way to the single room enclosed by a painted loggia establishing the fourth wall of the room of the Virgin and her devotee. The third set of windows looks out upon a golden Flemish landscape. Three sides of the room, including the implied side nearest the viewer, are pierced by openings. The visual construct is further elaborated in that, while the panels are physically in a single plane as they hang against the wall, they represent illusionistically the two perpendicular planes of the corner of a room. Since this corner coincides with the hinged joint of the two panels of the diptych, it could be recreated in actuality if the right wing of the diptych were pulled

forward ninety degrees. The perspective of the room would be broken, but van Nieuwenhove could then, like the viewer, adore the Virgin within her line of sight.

Situated at the edge of the loggia, the Virgin is almost as close to us as she is to the donor. Although she is confined by illusionistic perspective, the sanctity of her being is established by other compositional means. Her frontal, hieratic presence; her momentary gesture frozen for eternity by the idealizing force of the severe geometry of face, garments, limbs, fruit (and, by contrast, the donor's contemporary dress, portrait features, and hands folded in prayer) raise her to the level of icon—a separate, sacred personage beyond the Flemish moment in which we find her.

The specific Christian doctrines frequently associated with the window in the Renaissance gave way during the Baroque period in the seventeenth century to more general, moralizing themes represented in the guise of secular activities. The window still admits spiritual illumination, but the light often signifies human insight rather than divine revelation. The wisdom and foresight attributed to Rembrandt's *Scholar in His Study* and Vermeer's *Astronomer* and *Geographer* are expressed most explicitly by rays of light streaming into a darkened study. Sometimes the window was connected with the popular *vanitas* theme as a warning of the transience of life and the need to forgo worldly pleasures for the sake of ultimate salvation. For example, the window in Jan Steen's *The Miser and Death* (1654–56), rather than symbolically admitting divine light or truth, reveals death as a skeleton who knocks on the pane to collect his avaricious victim.

The best-known windows of the Baroque period may be those painted by Johannes Vermeer. Vermeer's windows often furnish the only means of escape from his dense, potentially claustrophobic spaces. Were it not for these windows, the very life would drain from many of these severe, domestic habitats, for their light is sometimes the only active force in these human still lives. Without breaking the stillness, the warm light gently stirs the atmosphere.

Most of Vermeer's windows appear on the oblique wall, hence he could retain the source of light, but avoid a potentially distracting, distant view. Nor does Vermeer depict large expanses of floor or entire rooms that line up easily with the pictorial frame, as did the Annunciation chamber of *The Mérode Altarpiece*. His pictures are limited to

12

a small corner of an even smaller world where women singly or with another figure move through familiar domestic rituals. The protagonists in such scenes as *Woman Pouring Milk*, *Woman Putting on Pearls*, or *Woman Reading a Letter* seek a window for the light necessary to perform their simple activities. The figure and the viewer are magnetically drawn toward the same source of illumination. Light animates the space as concentration animates the women. Vermeer's light, with or without the actual depiction of a window, gives intensity and direction to every pictorial event. Along with the severe geometry, reduced number of colors, and simplified form, the light also elevates a potentially mundane action to an ideal world beyond the woman and her temporary preoccupation.

Vermeer made the window a participant in many an intimate drama. In the *Officer and Laughing Girl* from about 1658 (illus. 7), the window lies along the same plane as the three-quarter profile of the girl. It opens to the world as she smiles across to the officer. Like the map on the wall and the cavalier at her table, the window beckons. Travel and romance remain imaginary: the window discloses no object from the outside world; the map graphically charts contemporary Holland, but is at best an abstract guide; and the sexual allusion suggested by the man's presence and the glass of wine is unrealized. Caught between map, man, and window, the girl is suspended in the realm of possibility. All three imply attendant discovery and perhaps danger; all question her protected world. The hinted pleasures contrast with those celebrated by her quiet domesticity, heretofore the familiar realm of this still-youthful woman. The encounter enlivens both girl and room, giving each an unsuspected vitality.

In contrast, the window of Vermeer's *A Young Woman Standing at a Virginal* from about 1673 is as closed, white, and formidable as the figure who stands erect to play.[6] The painting is a study in probity. All is upright and rectangular; the color is limited to cool blues and white. Eros unabashedly addresses the spectator and proclaims the beauty, not of wanton love, but of fidelity, as he holds aloft a card which displays the number one. The woman looks at us directly, head and face exposed, her attitude not the least bit shy or coy. This room suggests no illicit meetings, no indulgence in drink or aimless travel. The starched uprights of room and picture frame hold in check the sensuous pleasure of music and relaxation. The window concludes the

Illus. 6. HANS MEMLING, *Virgin and Child with Portrait of Martin van Nieuwenhove*, 1487, oil on wood, each panel: 17⁵⁄₁₆ × 13 inches (43.9 × 33 cms). Memlingmuseum, St. John's Hospital, Bruges

scheme: barred by a rectangular grid, emitting only the whitest of light, it participates not at all in seduction but in containment. It contrasts with the colored, circular leaded panes that accompany couples engaged in some sexually suggestive action in other Vermeer paintings.

As in earlier Flemish painting, art historians have discovered symbolic content hidden behind the seemingly secular surface of Vermeer's work. *A Young Woman Standing at a Virginal* is thought to be a pendant to *A Young Woman Seated at a Virginal*, which depicts a woman surrounded by symbols of love, one of which is a painting of a procuress. Hence the moral is played out through the opposition of the two types of women and the music they play: the lusty and the demure, the prostitute and the virgin, surely the emblems of profane and sacred love.

One cannot leave the religious symbolism of the window in the seventeenth century entirely in the hands of the Dutch moralists. Light, after all, became as powerful a force in the Baroque period as had perspective during the Renaissance. A common tool of almost every Baroque painter, light was no longer limited to the objective description of color or form. A momentary moving force, it was used at will to shape, obliterate, obscure, or illuminate. Even though light rarely streamed through the constricting frame of a fictive window in Baroque art, it dramatically symbolized the hand of divinity for such artists as Rembrandt, Caravaggio, and Zurbaran. In the apse of Saint Peter's behind the great *Cathedra Petri* (1657–66), Bernini even dared to improve the light of heaven by inserting yellow glass in an oval window so that the light that fell down upon the gilded throne of Saint Peter would arrive with its own, albeit artificial, golden glow.

Although often depicted by these earlier masters, the window remained largely incidental or complementary to the content of their work. Not so in the modern period. Beginning in the early nineteenth century with the German Romantics, the window became a subject in its own right.[7] The expression of longing for worlds other than those confining, unhappy places of the present found its perfect vehicle in the window. No longer the half-hidden oblique source of light that it was for Vermeer, the depicted window was made to parallel the picture surface, and its increased size dominated the center of the pictorial field. The window framed some other, wholly different, world. These German paintings set up a dramatic contrast between   13 an ordinary interior and its unexpected view. The stark room of the artist and, by implication, of the viewer opened onto a dreamlike landscape.

In two drawings made in 1806, Caspar David Friedrich represented his studio as a room without casts, flowers, draperies, or any of the paraphernalia usually depicted in artists' studios. The room is lifeless and sterile save for an enormous window that dominates each drawing. Rather than concentrate on the interior of his workshop, Friedrich portrayed its windows.

Some twelve years later, Friedrich introduced his wife into his studio space in a painting called *Woman at the Window* (illus. 10). She looks out of the window with her back to us, a mute, closed figure frozen against the window ledge. Outside, slim masts of ships drift down the River Elbe before a faint hedge of poplars. Unavailable to her, the active life exists only in the world of vision. Almost without physical substance, her body blends into the walls of the studio. The light surrounding her head suggests the mental release that the window supplies. The too distant landscape, without paths or bridges to suggest human progress, cannot be gained save through art and thought.

Using exactly the same format, Johan Dahl's *View of the Pillnitz Castle* has no figure and discloses only the reverie of a distant castle bathed in the glow of a pink sunset. Even though a tiny road traverses this landscape, it lies at a tremendous distance from the viewer. The inaccessible exterior realm will never come closer than its reflection on the inside of the pane of glass.

Illus. 7. JOHANNES VERMEER, *Officer and Laughing Girl*, circa 1658, oil on canvas, 19⅞ × 18⅛ inches (50.5 × 46 cms). Copyright The Frick Collection, New York

These romantic nineteenth-century window views, like those of the twentieth-century Surrealist René Magritte, lock the spectator into an empty space. The only means of exit is through the world of dreams. Quiet, solitude, and romantic longing permeate such works. The picture frame opens upon the first, earthly reality; the window on the next. As a picture within a picture, perspective is twice considered. Because there is usually a large break between the close, large scale of the interior and the distant, smaller (and sometimes unsettling) exterior view, the drama of conflicting perspectives enhances the duality of the near and far, both literally and figuratively. The sense of continuity that is usually found in Renaissance and Baroque perspective is intentionally broken. The disjunctive potential of the window now emerges. The two spaces are still held under rational control, but the possibility has arisen of a permanent separation or, alternatively, merging of the real and the imaginary.

When the artist represented his studio bereft of properties or even a model, as in these German paintings, the suggestion was that inspiration lay not outside, but inside man. No amount of academic training or drawing from nature could produce the necessary vision. The window in the studio as the source of light and inspiration gradually became a secular metaphor for the imagination.

The association of the window with the eye and the mind of the artist had its roots in the Renaissance. Borrowing from the ancient Greeks who called the eye the window of the soul, Leonardo repeated: "The eye, which is called the window of the soul, is the chief means whereby the understanding may most fully and abundantly appreciate the infinite works of nature."[8] In trying to prove that the art of painting should be one of the liberal arts rather than a craft, and that those who practice it are, or should be, equal in status to men of letters, Leonardo argued that the artist is a man of great intelligence, uniquely favored by God—in short, possessed of genius. The Romantic period took to the idea of genius with a vengeance, celebrating the individual, and his subjectivity, and his dreams as never before.

The image of the window was popular in poetry and art theory throughout the nineteenth century, but it became a dominant pictorial form again only at the end of the century, when the Symbolists, led by the poet Stéphane Mallarmé, took up the Romantics' interest in the theme. Many artists, such as Bonnard and Vuillard, adopted the domestic interior, often with windows, as a common subject.

In the late nineteenth century, as in the Renaissance, both the view through the window and the frame itself were reexamined. The Impressionists used the rectangular frame to locate their pictorial field, just as Alberti had. But instead of using the rectangle as a boundary for the perspectival system, they used the frame to organize and limit the subjects they sought in nature.[9] Although Impressionist painters frequently completed and reworked their paintings in the studio, their initial innovation lay in fixing their fleeting subject, a brief moment of experience, within nature's boundless expanse. The Impressionists reversed the Renaissance method of constructing a picture: they searched for their compositions in nature herself, not in a series of preconceived studies. As if looking through a viewfinder in a camera, they selected their pictorial subjects by imposing a given field upon a segment of the landscape.

Sometimes the rectangular format of the canvas was identical with that of an actual window. Early in the 1890s, Claude Monet painted multiple views of Rouen Cathedral in every color and at every time of day, often from exactly the same position—that established by the window of his rented room across the city square. He used the frame of an actual window to contain the inconstant light and color.

For the Impressionists the rectangular frame, initially based upon the window view, was a neutral device, of no dramatic significance to the internal construction of the work. The horizon line of the painted landscape usually simply paralleled the horizontal edges of the frame. For Edgar Degas and the Postimpressionists, working in the last two decades of the nineteenth century, the frame became an active compositional agent against which forms were pressed and cut. In painting after painting, moldings, floors, tables, and walls have no illusionistic beginning or end. They extend beyond the pictorial field and are often ruthlessly cropped by the four edges of the frame. Yet they do not seem incomplete, for they are secured by the frame and thereby subsumed into a larger abstract system. The frame counters and controls many of the interior compositional elements. In a revolutionary development at the very heart of modern painting, the two-dimensional composition (artifice), rather than the imagined view (reality), defines the unity of the work.

Illus. 8. EDGAR DEGAS, *La La at the Cirque Fernando, Paris,* 1879, oil on canvas, 46 × 30½ inches (116.8 × 77.4 cms). The Trustees of The National Gallery, London

In Degas' *La La at the Cirque Fernando, Paris* of 1879 (illus. 8), for example, all the struts of the opera house end at the edge of the canvas and are bounded by the frame. A potentially vast space is compressed into a segment made up of a tilted grid suspended from the four sides of the picture. La La's arm and body parallel the green supports. Because her figure is immobilized by the architectural armature, gravity seems to have been stripped of its force. Pictorially La La does not hang by her teeth, but is comfortably embedded in the two-dimensional series of supports which are fictively attached to the frame, rather than the floor and ceiling. In such works the frame is not a container to be looked through, but a major compositional device—an idea that was carried to much greater lengths by the Cubists in the early years of the twentieth century.

Adding full color to the Cubist vocabulary, Robert Delaunay painted, in 1912, a series of works called Simultaneous Windows.[10] Like many of the paintings within this group, *Windows* (page 33) uses the frame to establish the basic directions of the internal abstract system. The frame is also identical with the edges of the window portrayed. One seems to look through a window and at its reflected surface at the same time. The view combines the exterior scene of the Eiffel Tower with the surface of the window through which it is seen. In some of these window paintings Delaunay painted the frame itself as if it were an extension of the canvas. Whether canvas or painted frame, all the surfaces are controlled by a grid having the same orientation as the rectangular format. The internal shapes and colors are not those of the few recognizable objects. Even the famed silhouette of the Eiffel Tower is overpowered by the non-referential arcs that glide across the canvas. The exterior view and the window form a single object that transcends the limits of its subject as window, of its view of the city of Paris, and of the ordinary separation of frame and painted surface.

These restless shapes do not lie dormant on the canvas. Transparency and opacity, light and dark hue oscillate within the geometric structure, as if Newton's light-struck prism had come to life. Delaunay broke the conventions not only of focal-point perspective, but of local color, chiaroscuro, and the distinction between positive and negative space. The desire of artists to represent objects fixed in space with the accuracy perspective could afford died in the hands of the Cubists. For Delaunay the window was represented mainly by its fractured light. A system of interpenetrating forms results, not in one window but, as Delaunay would have it, in "simultaneous" windows.

In the early decades of the twentieth century, Henri Matisse also used the window in quite a different way—as a more conventional subject to join interior and exterior view. Sharing the heady Intimist view of Bonnard and Vuillard, he visualized the domestic interior as the center of a sensual world. Descendants of Vermeer's calm corners, Matisse's domestic spaces are drowned in textures, luminosity, and pattern of every imaginable kind. What the Madonna and Child were to van Eyck, the window was to Matisse. It afforded him an endless variation of subject: poetically celebrated in *Blue Window*, stern and forbidding in *French Window at Collioure* (illus. 14), lovingly varied and luminous through all the days of Nice. Often the view 15 through the painted window is so abstract or so unnatural that one is not certain whether it is actually a window or a framed picture, whether the image within is flat or implicitly three-dimensional. While Matisse insisted on the separation between window and room, he refuted the distinction between an interior and exterior view. Discussing his use of the window, Matisse stated: "Space is one unity from the horizon right to the interior of my work room. . . .The boat which is going past exists in the same space as the familiar objects around me, and the wall with the window does not create two different worlds."[11]

In Matisse's *Piano Lesson* of 1916 (illus. 12) walls, floor, and air are painted gray. The view through the window, seen as a long triangular green slash, has been flattened to conform to the patterns of the room and to the painted surface of the canvas. The distant, lush garden and the immaterial air share the opacity and flatness of the piano and wall. The difference between the exterior and the interior space is implied by a square opening, but within it the view clings to the surface of the window, denying the spectator access to the natural realm.

Profiting from the hard-earned pictorial freedom that slowly evolved during the last fifty years of the nineteenth century, Matisse and Delaunay began their mature styles unconditionally freed from the Renaissance view of reality as something seen through a window. For them, the painting need not have clearly recognizable objects as referents. The picture was the preserve of the artist tended by his imagination alone. The spectator must follow the artist into this world without external guides. When Matisse or Delaunay tantalize the viewer with such recognizable elements as a window or the Eiffel Tower, they force us to accept their tyranny twice over. A comfortable, known form is first acknowledged and then refuted before our eyes. Nothing behaves as we expect. Whether we want to or not, we must abandon our empirical view of an object and accept its new, unprecedented pictorial life.

In Matisse's *Red Studio* of 1911, for example, the walls and furniture are red, as is the very air itself. The world of artifice created by the painter—represented here by the numerous canvases on the floor and walls—is more real than the supposedly three-dimensional world of red objects, which lack all volume. The only reality is the world of the canvas or, in other words, the reality of the mind expressed by the artist's hand.

The picture as window culminates, as does so much else in the history of art, in Marcel Duchamp's *The Bride Stripped Bare by Her Bachelors, Even* (page 56). Made of glass, the picture itself has become, finally, a window. One set of images is painted or attached to the surface of the glass; others can be seen through it. Fused not fictively but actually, the real and painted world are at last one. Moreover, the stationary images attached to the glass are made in two, thought to be mutually exclusive, styles. The bachelors appear in the traditional perspectival manner of the Renaissance, the bride in the abstract Cubist mode. These two opposing constructs are joined with the real view, which is seen through the glass and is reflected on its surfaces. The constantly varying environment is absorbed into the picture but, of course, without being physically transformed. The environment cannot be contained by the static prison of the two-dimensional surface. Illusion and reality—those two never-to-be-married opposites—are wed, with each changing moment, far more ineluctably than the ever-ready bride and her host of impotent bachelors. But in the end the bride may love another, her maker Marcel. One translation of the title, based on a similarity of sound in French between "*même*" and "*m'aime*" reads: *The Bride Stripped Bare by Her Bachelors Loves Me*.[12] Like Pygmalion, Duchamp broke the boundary between art and life. The shattered window can no longer contain its image.

We need not wonder why at the turn of the twentieth century, the very moment when the Renaissance idea of the painting as a window view breathed its last, the window reemerged as a major pictorial subject. The window's shape is readily adaptable to painting's new two-dimensional requirements and easily echoes the increasingly prevalent grid construction. An appreciation of the significance of the four framing edges was clearly asserted by Hans Hofmann when he insisted that the first line on the canvas was in fact the fifth.

The window as a recognizable subject in art recalls images and ideas long associated with the mind and soul. It is one of the few symbols from the past that can still sustain a spiritual content. The studio with its requisite window personifies the artist's private world. Although the source of knowledge may no longer be a godhead but the subjective realm of the artist's mind, inspiration and creative force find still their symbol in the window and its light.

N O T E S

1. Leon Battista Alberti, *On Painting and On Sculpture: The Latin Texts of "De Pittura" and "De Statua"*, trans. Cecil Grayson (London 1972), I:19, p. 55.
2. See Carla Gottlieb's extensive writings on the history of the window in art.
3. Alberti, II:25, p. 61.
4. Cited by Erwin Panofsky, *Early Netherlandish Painting* (Cambridge, MA 1964), I, p. 144.
5. Ibid., p. 164.
6. For a discussion of these two works, see Madlyn Kahr, *Dutch Painting in the Seventeenth Century* (New York 1978), pp. 295–98.
7. See Lorenz Eitner, "The Open Window and the Storm Tossed Boat," *Art Bulletin*, 37, December 1955, pp. 281–90.
8. Leonardo da Vinci, *Leonardo da Vinci's Note-Books*, trans. Edward McCurdy (London 1906), p. 156.
9. For a discussion of the window in nineteenth-century theory and its repeated use by Monet, see Steven Z. Levine, "The Window Metaphor and Monet's Windows," *Arts Magazine*, 54, November 1979, pp. 98–104.
10. See Sherry Buckberrough, "The Simultaneous Content of Robert Delaunay's Windows," *Arts Magazine*, 54, September 1979, pp. 102–11.
11. Henri Matisse, *Matisse on Art*, ed. Jack D. Flam (New York 1973), p. 93.
12. Nicolas Calas, "The Large Glass," *Art in America*, 57, July–August 1969, p. 34.

16

*The retina is nothing but
a window behind which
stands a man.*
HENRI MATISSE[1]

AN ORDINARY WINDOW IS A simple enough object. But an ordinary window is imbued with an emotional life we give to it. Facing both out and in, the window is an invisible divide between our private and public selves. Through its transparent panes, we can watch light make shadow, day turn to night, and season give way to season. At times the clarity of the window's geometry provides a comprehensible form for the complexities of human experience, or focuses our awareness on unknown mysteries beyond our ken. As an aperture in an architectural wall, the window is similar to the eye, which links the visible world of nature to the invisible world of the mind. Ever since the ancient Greeks called the eye the window of the soul, images of windows have reappeared in art in infinite transformation.

The ancient window symbol became interwined with the window of perspective when Leon Battista Alberti formulated its practice during the Renaissance. Alberti called the painter's canvas "an open window through which the subject to be painted is seen."[2] Behind the transparent plane of Alberti's

Illus. 9. HENRI MATISSE, *Studio Quai St. Michel*, 1916, oil on canvas, 58¼ × 46 inches (147.9 × 116.8 cms). The Phillips Collection, Washington, DC

by Suzanne Delehanty

imaginary window, which was held in place by a prominent frame, the three-dimensional space of the real world could be depicted on the two-dimensional surface of the canvas. Suddenly, empowered by perspective, Renaissance painters were able to infuse the old symbols of the window with new veracity as apertures for sacred light or as screens between heaven and earth (illus. 3). In these windowed interiors sacred and profane events were captured in an illusion of immobile and timeless unity. The viewer, arrested in ideal stillness by perspective's all-controlling vanishing point, had a fixed place from which to contemplate the work of art. To re-create in painting the Renaissance vision of reality as a divinely ordered universe was an almost godlike human accomplishment and one which contributed to the elevation of the painter from humble craftsman to noble artist.

Renaissance perspective was such an extraordinary discovery that mathematicians elaborated its geometric complexities and artists developed its potential for mimetic representation for the next four hundred years. During the seventeenth century, however, in response to the Church's diminishing power, artists transposed the window symbol from a sacred to a secular motif in the new class of genre pictures celebrating the pleasures and foibles of daily life. Now light from the window gave form not only to divine wisdom, but to the thoughts of mortal men and women (illus. 7). In combination with the still life, the window also came to stand for the senses and the phenomenon of vision. Continuing on into the eighteenth century, artists used the window image to demonstrate their virtuosity in capturing the elusive drama of light itself.

With the rise of the Industrial Revolution in the nineteenth century, artists transformed the visible depictions of the window symbol and, as the century progressed, challenged Alberti's imaginary window, which framed the Renaissance view of reality. In the century's first decades the German Romantic painters seized the window symbol from its oblique position in painting and moved it front and center to make it the subject of the artist.[3] Since the window was an ancient metaphor for the eye carried forward in literature, treatises on art, and even Dürer's remarkable portraits (illus. 11), it expressed the Romantics'   17 growing belief in the artist's inspired originality. Theirs was the power to call forth new paradises from the imagination. Daring as the Romantic painter's new window was, it remained submerged in the hierarchy of academically sanctioned subjects in art throughout most of the century, although its image coursed through the poetry of the age.

In contrast, Alberti's imaginary window and the entire apparatus of Renaissance perspective landed in the middle of the debates about the truth of artistic representation, when, at mid-century, photography held up to painting a new standard of pictorial veracity.[4] Expectations for the image presented by the camera's eye were shaped, in fact, by the very foundations of the painting that this picture-making machine modified, altered and, ultimately, threatened. In the 1860s painters defied the time-honored concept of art as imitation and flattened the human figure to satisfy the needs of their two-dimensional canvases. It was as if the force of painters clashing with the camera and the Industrial Revolution had pushed the geometric system of Renaissance perspective against the inside of Alberti's imaginary window to dislodge the vanishing point, wipe away chiaroscuro, and free the artist's hitherto suppressed colors and brushstrokes, leaving only the frame and the grid that had guided illusionistic renderings for centuries. This tension between the surface and edges of a painting and the illusion of depth, between abstraction and representation, increased in the 1890s with the Symbolist painters, who considered painting "a creation of our spirit for which nature is only the occasion."[5]

Illus. 10. CASPAR DAVID FRIEDRICH, *Woman at the Window*, circa 1818, oil on canvas, 17⅜ × 14⅝ inches (44 × 37.1 cms). Staatliche Museen, Preussischer Kulturbesitz, Nationalgalerie, Berlin

Freed from the hallowed conventions of perspective, window images began to reappear in painting for the first time since the Romantic period. From Edouard Manet in the 1860s to Claude Monet in the 1870s to Odilon Redon in the 1880s to the intimate interiors of Pierre Bonnard and Edouard Vuillard (page 36) at the turn of the century, images of windows took the place of the implied views through Alberti's imaginary window.

At the beginning of the twentieth century, the window offered the pioneers of modernism a way to mediate between the openly acknowledged fiction of the flat canvas and the exhilarating, if unsettling, overthrow of perspective. It was not simply a pictorial convention that was removed; the break marked the collapse of the whole Newtonian construct of a measurably ordered universe. Scientists and philosophers had now come to believe that reality was an ever-changing continuum in which man's physical sensations and the processes of the mind were not separate, but inextricably bound in perpetual exchange. The early modernists set out to discover a way of presenting an entirely new understanding of reality, shaped by the elusive resonance between the eye and the mind, the past and the present.

The capacity of the window to assume various forms from the tangible world and the realm of art made the window a potent and adaptable image for the creation of a new vision in art. In these new views of reality, artists would draw inspiration from existing models of the window in the ordinary world, in poetry, and in art. Some artists would use the window's geometry to create new pictorial order and spaces to mediate between abstraction and figuration. Others would adopt the window to study the long-standing concerns of light and human emotion, while others would enlist the window in the liberation of color and in speculations on the enterprise of art: its conventions, history, and the artistic process.

The window was a perfect subject for Henri Matisse. From *The Open Window* of 1905 ablaze in Fauvist color to the startling mystery of *French Window at Collioure* of 1914 to *The Egyptian Curtain* of 1948 (illus. 14, 19), the simple geometry of the window yielded its pleasures to Matisse's remarkable innovations in color and his light-drenched creations of opulent, space-giving hues and sensuous touch. To acknowledge the correspondence he deeply felt between the canvas and the window, Matisse emphasized again and again the similarities of their structures—for example, in *The Open Window* and in *The Green Pumpkin* from about 1920 (illus. 13), in which the bold black upright member of the window's casement and even the dangling pull of the window shade echo the stretcher's unseen vertical support. Matisse recorded his affection for the simple structure: "I thus have before my eyes the back of the frame with keys. It is so well proportioned, so neat, in lovely natural wood, that it is a work of art."[6] For Matisse and other twentieth-century painters the canvas and the window were analogues for the artist's imagination and their desire to mediate between and, at the same time, reveal the duality of the object seen and its pictorial representation. A threshold between inside and outside space, the window embodied artists' growing awareness of the infinitely complex transmission of their inner thoughts to the outer world through the palpable substance of paint and canvas.

18

The relation of the window to the canvas is linked to the artist's studio, a theme Matisse transformed and elaborated in such works as *The Red Studio* of 1911 and *Studio, Quai St. Michel* of 1916 (illus. 9). Here, tall windows separate the outside world from the artist's work place. The nude model, formerly held behind Dürer's perspectival grid (illus. 1), reclines beneath three pictures within the picture, which symbolize the levels of the painter's artifice. The canvas upon which the artist, momentarily absent, is working rests on an easel. Matisse's subject is not the model, but rather the artist's realm: the intricate interconnections among window, model, color, canvas, and artist. The entire field of perception is presented to us in what is both the artist's view and his fiction. The artist's studio, to which the window and the canvas are allied, was Matisse's empire, the sacred space of artistic creation deeded to the artists of our century by the painters and the poets of the last.

Around 1908 both Picasso and Braque took a more radical approach to the window. In bold attack on the last vestiges of perspective, the inventors of Cubism in fact abandoned the window image. In their first experiments they dispelled it from their painting precisely because of its power to elicit illusionistic space, which was the very reason Matisse adopted and celebrated the window motif throughout his life. Nevertheless, the semblance of space was not easily relinquished. The Cubist experiments of Picasso and Braque were at the forefront of Robert Delaunay's imagination when, in 1912, he set out to discover pure painting in his bedazzling series of Simultaneous Windows (page 33). To offset the Cubists' total disdain for the illusion of space, Delaunay fused the window image, a natural grid, in breathtaking union with canvas and spectrum of pure color. In this series Delaunay merged a view of the visible world—sunlight and the curves of moving curtains—with an evocation of the mystical window of revelatory light extolled by the Romantic poets. This cycle of paintings brought Delaunay so alarmingly close to total abstraction that he turned back to the comfort of recognizable subjects. But in the brilliant grids of the Simultaneous Windows, Delaunay achieved a remarkable expression of the movement and vibrancy of the world inside and outside ourselves.

In 1915 Juan Gris, an early Cubist innovator, also turned to the window image. In *The Table in Front of the Window* (page 35), one of a series of works devoted to the theme from

Illus. 11. (Detail) ALBRECHT DÜRER, *Philip Melanchthon*, 1526, engraving, 6⅞ × 5⅛ inches (17.6 × 13 cms). Grunwald Center for Graphic Arts, Wight Art Gallery, University of California at Los Angeles

1921, Gris set out to unite the dissected objects and flattened space of Cubism with the suggestive space and light of the open window. His interest in the window image was not solely formal. He was also attracted to the still life before the window, a traditional theme and long an emblem for the human senses. For Gris the open window was a subject which reinforced the Cubists' intent to portray, with shifting forms and evocative images, the interaction between the mind and the senses of sight, sound, smell, and touch.

Marcel Duchamp responded to the Cubists' attack on perspective and the convention of the window image in his ironic studies of the nature of artistic representation. In 1915 Duchamp began, as he described it, the rehabilitation of perspective in *La Mariée mise à nu par ses célibataires, même (le Grand Verre); The Bride Stripped Bare by Her Bachelors, Even (The Large Glass)*, which was completed in New York in 1923 (illus. 15 and page 56). Rather than use the traditional canvas and stretcher, Duchamp used sheets of glass bought from a hardware store and mounted in a frame. Freestanding, *The Large Glass* is not dependent on a wall, the usual place for both an ordinary window and a painting. The viewer can walk around it and look through the glass from either side or catch shadowy reflections of objects and motion behind him. Instead of opening onto the view prescribed by Alberti, *The Large Glass* contains a diagram of the two opposing and equally abstract conventions of representation. The lower half, where the machinelike bachelors, coffee grinders, and eye charts reside, is rendered according to the laws of perspective. In the upper half, the bride's domain, a series of veil-like squares, conceived without perspective and in the Cubist mode, appear to float.

The materials and artistic conventions chosen for *The Large Glass* are intricately bound to its meaning, layer by layer. The images in the lower part of the window project onto the floor behind the work. Without the usual support of an opaque canvas to affirm the illusion of the artist's rendering, these objects contradict and ultimately deny the semblance of volume given them by Duchamp. The metal crossbar coincides with, and simultaneously cancels, the vanishing point to ensure that the bride will never succumb to the bachelors' advances. She is an ideal, evoking representations of the Virgin Mother floating in apotheosis in the sacred space of religious paintings of the past. Set apart, the bride stands for a pure and innocent world, the Eden before the Fall sought by the Romantic poets whom   19

Duchamp admired. The bachelors are mere impostors—contraptions spawned in an endless stream of look-alikes by the machine age. The knowing bachelors understand the world and its ways, its inventions and modes of representation. They belong to Eden after the Fall, to an innocence lost to consciousness. Despite their imprisonment in a secular space, the bachelors nevertheless seek physical union with the bride—the moment of love when all differences between male and female vanish in the mystical ecstasy of passion. Duchamp understood that the quest is futile, for male and female are in eternal opposition. The bachelors' desire is as impossible as the artist's yearning to reconcile irreconcilable differences between illusion and reality, or to extend them into another dimension of apparition and appearance, as Duchamp had endeavored to do. With *The Large Glass*, the first of a number of speculative windows that would have an enormous influence on the century, Duchamp upended the conventional role of the work of art from an immobile and timeless object viewed by a passive onlooker to a fictive system for endless speculation by a mobile, thinking viewer.

The contradictions posed by the window perplexed René Magritte as well. In the twenties and thirties, while some of the Surrealists turned to biomorphic abstraction, Magritte used perspective and a meticulous realism to question the view of reality these artistic conventions had formerly upheld. Through such a contradiction, he set out to uncover the uncertainty disguised by custom and habit in order to present a view of reality that could not be truly discerned by either the mind or the senses. Disquietude arises in Magritte's work from such impossibilities as a huge green apple occupying a room with lambent light as pregnant with imminent events as van Eyck's (page 52, illus. 4). Flat images with unmatched names appear on the opaque windowpanes of *La clef des songes (The Key of Dreams)* of 1936 (page 53). In *Le soir qui tombe (Evening Falls)* of 1964 (page 70), the broken glass reveals that the painted image of a canvas and the depiction of the window view are one and the same. This picture within a picture is Magritte's ironic repartee to Alberti's concept of painting as an open window. The difference between the object seen and its depiction haunts *Evening Falls* and a series of similar window paintings from the thirties called *La condition humaine (The Human Condition)*. Of the window and its dilemma Magritte wrote: "In front of a window seen from inside a room, I placed

Illus. 12. HENRY MATISSE, *Piano Lesson*, 1916, oil on canvas, 96½ × 83¾ inches (245.1 × 212.7 cms). The Museum of Modern Art, New York, Mrs. Simon Guggenheim Fund

a painting representing exactly that portion of the landscape covered by the painting. . . . For the spectator it was both inside and outside the room within the painting and outside in the real world. We can see outside ourselves, and at the same time we have a representation of it in ourselves."[7] This disjunction of means, which would be taken up by artists in the sixties, enabled Magritte to heighten the abstraction of his inquiry.

At the time Magritte was using the window to question the nature of artistic representation, a number of artists on both sides of the Atlantic explored, as artists long had done, the emotive and formal qualities of the window image. In Europe, Mark Chagall framed his fantasy of a remembered courtship in the sky beyond his flower-filled window in *Dream Village* of 1929 (page 34), while in the United States, Edward Hopper painted windows based on observations of familiar buildings and streets. Hopper's windows and their light contribute to the emotional quality he sought in his art. Rendered with architectural solidity, the light in *Night Windows* of 1928 and *The Barber Shop* of 1931 (pages 75, 71), for instance, shapes the psychological currents in these scenes of lonely city life. Like a cinematographer, Hopper cropped the scene of *Night Windows* to peep into a young woman's bedroom. We become unseen observers looking from our second-story window through outdoor darkness into the warm lamplit room of an unknowing girl. The position Hopper has given to us greatens the drama. On the side of one window, a lace curtain caught in an eddy of air quickens our unease in a manner far more unnerving than the overt suggestiveness of Balthus' haunting classical paintings of windows and female figures from the same period (illus. 18, page 69).

By contrast, the mood of Marsden Hartley's *Sea Window, Tinker Mackerel* of 1942 (page 84), painted shortly before his death, is one of quiet resignation. The still life before an open window, a theme Hartley often returned to in times of trial, is a study of the containment and expansiveness of the window's form. The window's transom defines a dark, compressed interior space. At the same time, the window frames a landscape with a vast sky of light and clouds so lovingly painted that the window and its view become a composition within a composition.

For Milton Avery, also, the window's rectangular shape was an inviting expanse for paint. In the forties, inspired by the example of Matisse and Picasso, Avery began to explore

20

color in such works as *Seated Girl with Dog* of 1944 (page 93)—no longer for the actual description of objects from his domestic environment, but rather to examine the abstract relations of color. Here the window opens to a vibrant orange plane where Avery's incised marks bring a seemingly distant cityscape from the whiteness of his canvas. A deep purplish blue wall counterpoints the brilliant abstraction of the window view and enlivens the play of reds, blues, and pinks in the young girl's form. Through his masterful interaction of colors, Avery achieved a new, flat pictorial space within the figurative tradition.

During the 1940s, the window in American art took an elemental form. This simplified form revealed the intent, among progressive artists of the period, to discover a new beginning through the most distilled pictorial means. They sought to create equivalents for the uncertainty of modern life. Invigorated by the artists and intellectuals escaping to New York from the war in Europe, American artists shed the provincialism of the depression years. The creative moment, the myth, the human dilemma, became the center of interest for this circle of artists who, by the end of the decade, would be called Abstract Expressionists.

During 1941 Adolph Gottlieb and Mark Rothko worked together to free themselves from the hold of figuration and spatial illusion in order to put painting, as Gottlieb said, "at the beginning of seeing."[8] Much as the Cubists had done in their revolutionary break from perspective, Gottlieb and Rothko squeezed the space-giving power of the window image from their work made in the 1930s

Illus. 13. HENRI MATISSE, *The Green Pumpkin*, circa 1920, oil on canvas, 30½ × 24½ inches (77.4 × 62.2 cms). Museum of Art, Rhode Island School of Design. Anonymous gift

(pages 42, 97).[9] Both artists moved even farther away from the recognizable subject matter of their mentor Milton Avery as they investigated more deeply the ideas of Cubism and biomorphic Surrealism. Gottlieb's search led him to invent his windowlike pictographs, compositions with the all-over order of the Cubists' grid. He continued to refine these ideas in such works as *Evil Omen* of 1946 (page 43). Rothko's quest led to the mythological studies (page 97) in which he flattened out space, but maintained the boundaries of the canvas by painting borders along the framing edge. By the fifties Rothko had eliminated all identifiable images to create pure pictorial space and light with translucent washes of pigment—cerulean blue, the darkest of maroons, drifts of pure white. Yet there is still a suggestion of the framing edge in *Old Gold over White* of 1956 (page 96). A faint apparition of a window seems to hover on the vertical

expanse of the canvas, which is large enough to surround and hold for our contemplation the artist's equivalent of timeless light and limitless space. It is as if Rothko had made us the lonely viewer in German Romantic painting who gazed out the window at a world created by the artist's imagination (illus. 10).

The small barred rectangle in Robert Motherwell's *Spanish Picture with Window* of 1941 (page 41) rests amid a web of hand-drawn horizontal and vertical lines which seem to extend beyond the canvas into infinity. Gone is the frame that once held the window of Renaissance art firmly in place. While painting became a flat open field, edges became an increasingly important concern for Motherwell and his contemporaries, much as they would during the next two decades for the formalist painters. In Motherwell's *Spanish Elegies* of the fifties, the simple geometry of the window image, his symbol for the power of reason, moved in stately measure along with the oval form, his symbol for the irrational force of human passion. The window image became a forceful presence again in the late sixties. According to Motherwell, he spotted the back of a small canvas leaning against a larger painting one day in the studio. Taken by the proportions, he drew the outline of the smaller canvas' top and sides on the larger canvas. The possibilities of these three lines within the four edges and the richness of color led him to renew the theme of the window and the wall and his deep appreciation of Matisse in the *Opens*, a series that includes *The Garden Window* of 1969 (page 40). *The Garden Window* is Motherwell's direct response to the view of a lush landscape from a new studio in Connecticut. In the *Opens* Motherwell sought, like Rothko, Gottlieb and the other Abstract Expressionists, to unify the artist's inner world with the mythic continuum of time and space.

The dichotomy between the artist's inner life and external reality animates Hans Hofmann's drawings of his studio windows from the war years (page 87) as well as his later *Magenta and Blue* of 1950 (page 88), in which a barely recognizable still life on a table before a window is flattened out in what Hofmann called pure plastic creation. The European-born Hofmann, a redoubtable force among the Abstract Expressionists and master teacher of generations of American artists, appreciated the ability of the window to function as an expanse for color suggestive of space while maintaining the flatness of the canvas. During 21 the fifties the power of abstraction took greater hold of Hofmann. In 1960 he distilled the windows of medieval cathedrals into rectangular planes of blue, red, and green on a pure yellow field pulsating in *Auxerre, France. St. Etienne's Glorious Light Emanated by Its Windows, as Remembered* of 1960 (page 89). This painting joins the ancient association of the window and light in a new way, and embodies one of Hofmann's beliefs: "Color in itself is light. In nature light creates color; in pictures color creates light."[10]

Although the innovation and authority of Abstract Expressionism dominated the fifties, the windows found in the work of other artists of the period demonstrate the flexibility of their form in a wide range of artistic expressions. As a young artist in postwar Paris, Ellsworth Kelly made a number of forthright objects recording the window and its light. Kelly's recollection of *Window, Museum of Modern Art, Paris* of 1949 (page 44) is revealing: "In October of 1949 in the Museum of Modern Art in Paris I noticed the large windows between the paintings interested me more than the art exhibited. I made a drawing of the window and later in my studio, I made what I considered my first object. From then on painting as I had known it was finished for me."[11] The object is, in fact, a relief. Composed of two canvases set into a black wooden frame, it has the same proportions but is smaller than the actual museum window that inspired its fabrication. Three glazing bars divide the lower half of the window and physically cross over the canvas to cast actual, not painted, shadows on the recessed gray surface. Neither wholly painting nor wholly sculpture, *Window* was prophetic of Kelly's own future work as well as of minimal art and the hybrids of painting and sculpture that would intrigue artists in the next two decades. In France Kelly came to rely on his powers of observation to discover possibilities in ordinary things: an awning, a roadside sign, pavement, a window. Light falling through an irregularly shaped window in a banded pattern made by crossed telephone wires, for instance, led to Kelly's *Window V* of 1950 (page 45). A craftsman's thumbnail sketch set Kelly's mind going and emerged rethought in *Black and White (Carpenter's Window)* of 1955 (page 46). The apparent straightforwardness of this work belies its complexity. Kelly divided his canvas into two black rectangles in such a way that the whole and its parts question one another. Does the white framing edge rest on top of the two black panes, as a nighttime window might appear? Or do the black

Illus. 14. HENRI MATISSE, *French Window at Collioure*, 1914, oil on canvas, 45¹¹/₁₆ × 34⅝ inches (115.9 × 87.9 cms). Musée National d'Art Moderne, Paris

rectangles rest on a white surface? What is shape, and what is space?

If Ellsworth Kelly is a maker of factual objects, Joseph Cornell, who was inspired by the Surrealists in the 1930s, was a maker of boxes of poetic reverie. Kelly's windows are grounded in fact, but Cornell's observatories, hotels, and window facades from the early fifties float in illusion. There are several layers of windowed artifice, for instance, in *Observatory Columba Carrousel* of 1953 (page 79). A real pane of glass, Cornell's own version of Alberti's imaginary window, ensures that the space behind it is ideal and timeless. A second window lies behind the first framed, protective transparent plane. This window opens onto a view of a starry sky in shorthand approach to the order of Renaissance perspective. A mirror, the window's illusory counterpart, is placed at right angles to the inner window and reflects the light of long-extinct stars from a far-distant past into a vastness which would have delighted the nineteenth-century Romantic poets. It was these same poets who pointed the way for Cornell's tabletop universe and white-window facade (page 78), his homage to Mondrian, in which a grid and mirrors extend Cornell's window views into infinity. The very small-ness of Cornell's windowed worlds makes the immensity of his cosmos all the grander.

Another expression appears in the windows of Richard Diebenkorn. He turned away from the gestural power of Abstract Expressionism in the mid-fifties to pursue the seemingly less daring course of figurative painting, a path already taken and steadfastly maintained by Milton Avery, Fairfield Porter, and Jane Freilicher (pages 92, 48, 49). Diebenkorn understood, as did Avery, Porter, Freilicher—and Matisse before them—that figuration is abstract. Like them, he was attracted by the window's capacity to invoke both interior and exterior space. In *Woman in a Window* of 1957 (page 72), pictorial events move in balanced contrast. The geometry of the window and tabletop is set against the warm hues and curving forms of the young woman and her upholstered chair; the space-giving blues and the diagonals of the window's edges provoke a lively dialogue between the pensive figure and the open window. The edges of the canvas vibrate with painterly incidents which seem to weave into and unite with the window's vertical transom, where the vanishing point of perspective might once have held us.

The window's ease in oscillating between figuration and

22

abstraction led Diebenkorn in the late sixties in another bold new direction. After more than a decade of figurative work, he returned to abstraction in the *Ocean Park* series. The brilliant light of Southern California that he saw from his studio window impressed him profoundly, as did a renewed contemplation of Matisse. The near abstraction of Matisse's *French Window at Collioure* of 1914 (illus. 14) astonished him as well as Motherwell and many other artists when it was first shown publicly in the 1960s. In his *Ocean Park* paintings, Diebenkorn reduced the window's transom to horizontal and vertical lines which thread in changing weights around the canvas' framing edge, intersect diagonals, and cross over layers of subtle, varying color, such as the blues and greens in *Ocean Park #111* of 1978 (page 73). Deftly applied paint—here fluid, there dense—quivers with controlled spontaneity in window views that frame the endless sky and sea and the painter's process.

By the late fifties, newspapers, comics, ads, billboards, radio, film, and television had flooded the natural environment. Just as the Industrial Revolution of the nineteenth century had driven Romantic painters to portray windows opening onto paradises of the imagination, the mass-produced sameness of the Media Age stimulated a response from artists. The windows in the art of the late fifties and sixties demonstrate a variety of approaches to the change from a natural to an essentially man-made landscape. The formalist painters, the heirs to Abstract Expressionism, would turn away from all references to the window and its space as well as the environment, whether natural or man-made; others would accept the media landscape and enlist the art of the French modernists or the irony of Duchamp and Magritte to transform their window views.

When Jasper Johns pulled down and affixed over his canvas an ordinary dime-store window shade, he shut out from the painting all notions of cosmic or illusory space. His *Shade* of 1959, which pursues the same area of inquiry as Duchamp's *The Large Glass* and Magritte's *The Key of Dreams* (pages 56, 53), completely hides Alberti's open window to ask about the view that is not given and how the view is to be seen. The window that reappeared in Johns' *Studio 2* of 1966 (page 93) begins to reveal the nature of his speculations. The standard-sized windows in *Studio 2* are impressions made by Johns from the real windows in his work space. The casements left the imprint of rectangles; the glazing bars marked the white grids. Joyful secondary

Illus. 15. MARCEL DUCHAMP, *The Bride Stripped Bare by Her Bachelors, Even. Installed in Katherine Dreier's house, Milford, Connecticut*, 1915–23, oil and lead wire on glass, 109¼ × 69⅛ inches (277.5 × 175.5 cms). Philadelphia Museum of Art, bequest of Katherine S. Dreier

colors, unusual for Johns, record the artist's sensuous pleasure in paint. The ruler in the upper right hand corner confirms the window's scale and reminds us of the tools artists commonly use. Johns has brought us right into his working process. His windows and canvas are as close to us as they were to him in the making. By contrast, in the studio of Matisse (illus. 9) we are given, so to speak, a place on the far side of the atelier, where the painter's canvas and nude model are beyond our reach. The window and the artist's depiction of his canvas position us in relation to his model. In Johns, there is no model, and the real window's image and the canvas are one, and record the artist's process.

The inquiry made by Johns' *Shade* continues in the series of provocative window shades made by Robert Moskowitz in the early sixties. Moskowitz's *Untitled* of 1962 (page 98) is fringed and is as double edged as the Johns *Shade*. Considered half closed, it affirms the opacity of the canvas to which it is laminated. Looked at half opened, it exposes the real space between the painting and the wall as well as the stretcher bars, which once supported the illusion of space. By choosing a flat, commonplace domestic contrivance from a plethora of faceless manufactured goods, Moskowitz revealed a debt to Marcel Duchamp. Duchamp's presence and writings had gained the increased attention of an entire new generation of artists who were ready to embrace and to question the contemporary world.

Tom Wesselmann's *Great American Nude #35* of 1962 (page 50) combines a still life before a window with the equally traditional themes of the nude and the landscape. This mixed media assemblage revels in an abundance of diverse images made for the consumer. A latticed window, which resembles those of seventeenth-century Dutch painting or Vuillard's turn-of-the-century interiors, offers a view, not of a lush garden, but of flowered wallpaper. Rather than a painted sweep of organdy gauze, an actual polka-dotted curtain hangs limply at the window. A mass-produced Mona Lisa and a pin-up girl from a *Playboy* centerfold, altered by Wesselmann to resemble Matisse's late odalisques, have replaced the pensive women of Vermeer's interiors. Real beer and soda bottles complete with brand labels stand where one might expect to find the dissected objects of Cubist still lifes, such as the ones created by Juan Gris in 1921 (page 35). In other works from the series of *Great American Nudes*, Wesselmann's windows open onto picture-postcard views of snow-topped moun-   23 tains, silhouettes of tropical palm trees, or pictures of shiny new red cars. Even real TV sets appear in front of some of Wesselmann's windows to suggest, as Shigeko Kubota would in the 1970s (page 54), that the electronic box has replaced the window as the mediator between our inner world and the world outside. It transmits a new illusion of reality, the American dream.

Roy Lichtenstein's windows offer a more austere investigation of the artifacts of our media-oriented society. In 1961 Lichtenstein abandoned the subjectivity of Abstract Expressionism and adopted the impersonal style and subjects of mass media. In *Curtains* of 1962 (page 82), which was based on ads for furnishing the American dream house, and in *Stretcher Frame with Cross Bars II* of 1968 (page 82), a comment on the art-making process, Lichtenstein used the bold outlines of advertising and the Benday dots of commercial printing to remodel already flattened objects into modern icons. In *Stretcher Frame* Lichtenstein advanced the self-conscious practice of Wesselmann and other contemporary artists of appropriating images from their studios, popular culture, and the fine arts. By selecting the painter's stretcher as his subject, Lichtenstein relied on the connection in the viewer's mind between this apparently anonymous image, the window, and the depictions of canvases placed near windows presented in masterpieces by Velázquez, Caspar David Friedrich, Matisse (illus. 9), and Picasso (page 85). The anonymity of Lichtenstein's means only heightens the impact of the image in the mind of the observer—particularly observers conditioned by the Abstract Expressionists to regard the painter's canvas with reverence.

The pioneers of modernism unleashed and put into motion the fictive circuit of art that continues to engage Lichtenstein in such a rigorously composed work as *Paintings Near Window* of 1983 (page 66). In this laconic exercise of visual wit the artist echoed Matisse's *Red Studio* and Magritte's *The Human Condition*. Even the title of Lichtenstein's *Paintings Near Window* extends the metaphor of the artist's canvas and the window. Within the 1983 painting, a frilly curtain is pulled back to reveal a graphic rendition of the silhouette of a blue palm tree in stylized sway over a tropical landscape. It is not an eden, but a composite of Lichtenstein's earlier work. Next to this romantic view is an image of the all-over gestural compositions of Abstract Expressionism. It is, in fact, a quotation from Lich-

Illus. 16. MARCEL DUCHAMP, *Fresh Widow*, 1920 (third version), miniature French window, painted wood frame, and eight panes of glass covered with black leather, 30½ × 20⅞ × 3⁵⁄₁₆ inches (77.4 × 53 × 8.4 cms). Indiana University Art Museum. Partial gift of Mrs. William Conroy

tenstein's *Brushstroke* series of the sixties. Both images are stepped back from reality many times over. They exchange identities in layers of illusion, thereby offering a prospect of the artist's history and the tradition of painting.

The ease with which the window suits both painting and sculpture, the ordinary and the mysterious, led Christo to build to scale a series of storefronts (page 90) in the mid-sixties with materials salvaged from urban-renewal sites or bought in a hardware store, much as Duchamp had done for *The Large Glass* some forty years before. But Christo removed his storefronts from their ordinary place on a city street and placed them in the unexpected context of a gallery or museum, where visitors in the mid-sixties still expected to see bronze sculptures mounted on pedestals and framed paintings hanging on walls. Christo's life-sized storefronts establish a direct physical relation with viewers accustomed to seeing their own reflection in store windows. Again we are confounded. The windows of the storefronts are shrouded with brown paper, not only to render opaque what by definition is transparent, but to contradict the function of store windows as a display area for commercial products. By covering the ordinary window, Christo invited us to uncover, as Duchamp and Magritte had done earlier, the disquieting currents beneath everyday experience.

Underlying Richard Artschwager's seemingly simple window images is a sleight of mind which turns reality into illusion and illusion into reality to jar us—by a means different from Christo's—out of our habitual way of seeing and knowing the world. In his *Untitled* of 1966 (page 58), a hybrid painting and sculpture made of formica, Artschwager has given us, on one level, all the attributes of an ordinary window: frame, cross-supports, even chamfered edges. The object, however, is not opaque and its cross-supports are so enlarged that its practical function as a window is denied. Depending on where we stand, we are barred from a view of the world without or the room within. On another level, *Untitled* has all the attributes of a work of art: imposing frame, perspectival space, and horizontal format suggestive of a landscape. Half painting, half sculpture, it even hangs on a wall, as one expects a traditional painting to do. Like the work of Christo and Lichtenstein, Artschwager's piece questions habits that have been shaped by art's conventions. The bulky cross-supports of *Untitled* call attention to the plane of Alberti's imaginary window, but the illusory view is not

24

there. The space receding behind the picture plane is instead an actual three-dimensional creation made not to focus our eyes on the view, but to focus our minds on the process of perception.

Although by tradition a painter's image, the window attracted a number of adventurous artists working in new sculptural forms and eager to establish a vital relation with the viewer. Real windows from the ordinary world of tract houses, gas stations, and shops have fascinated George Segal since the late 1950s, when he abandoned abstract painting to make life-sized plaster casts of actual men and women in commonplace environments. A persistent fixture in these environments, the window allowed Segal to combine painting's two-dimensional plane with sculpture's three-dimensional volumes, and in its geometry to wed his admiration for Mondrian's pure abstraction to the expressiveness of Matisse. From pieces made in 1961 to *Girl Sitting against a Wall II* of 1970 (page 81) to recent works, Segal has used the window's familiarity and human scale to put viewer and cast figures on an equal footing in a common space. By pairing window and figure, Segal defined the difference between the viewer's real space and the sculpture's space. The distance encourages us to see ordinary human situations afresh. Like the window in Hopper's paintings, the window in Segal's tableaux frames his haunting figures and calls to our attention unseen thoughts and longings under the skin of the familiar scenes of daily life.

The window, a natural architectural foil for the human figure, attracted David Hockney as well. In the 1960s Hockney chose to combine his interest in portraiture, classical perspective, and light—artistic pursuits little esteemed by the formalists of the sixties—with the modernist demand for pictorial flatness. In *Henry Geldzahler and Christopher Scott* of 1968–69 (page 68), the culmination in a series of double portraits of men modeled after Renaissance scenes of the Annunciation, Hockney gave the window symbol a new meaning and altered the fundamental rules of perspective. On the one hand, he used classical perspective in the Renaissance manner to establish the hieratic position of Henry Geldzahler, a well-known curator of contemporary art, who sits before a window. On the other hand, he denied perspective its power to create the illusion of space by hiding the vanishing point behind Geldzahler's head. Had Hockney made the portrait completely flat in the modern tradition, he would have declared the factual reality of his

Illus. 17. (Detail) Edward Kienholz and Nancy Reddin Kienholz, *Deep Purple Rage*, 1981, mixed media, 60 × 48 × 30 inches (152.4 × 121.9 × 76.2 cms). L. A. Louver Gallery, Venice, California

canvas and support. The window image and the altered perspective allowed the artist to maintain, with great wit, a desired modicum of illusion. The double portrait, then, is Hockney's challenge to the Renaissance masters as much as it is to the formalists.

The break from formalism and Pop Art in the 1970s opened the way for artists to use the window in more diverse ways, encompassing artists' traditional interest in the window as a reflective surface, innovations in joining painting and sculpture, and the new illusionism of the eighties. Richard Estes and other Photo-Realists, who emerged visibly amid the pluralism of the 1970s, were captivated by windows, particularly the large expanses of commercial plate glass that they depicted according to laws of perspective. Even in Pop Art's heyday in the 1960s, Estes had remained committed to perspective and its spatial illusion. By 1970, gathering inspiration from the photographs of Atget and the urban vistas of Canelletto, he began to concentrate on views of city streets and windowed facades. He was drawn to the abstract possibilities of such windows—their strong horizontal and vertical lines and layers of transparent planes, such as those he depicted in *Diner* of 1971 (page 62). Additionally, the windows of commercial buildings offered Estes a way to counter the formalists' doctrine in order to pursue the challenge of portraying what he called painting's double life: the record of an observed view, and a flat abstraction. The same possibilities for abstraction and layers of reflected images fascinated Don Eddy in his series of showrooms in the early seventies—supermarkets, jewelry shops, and shoe shops. In Eddy's *New Shoes* of 1973 (page 63), for example, windows are framing devices and reflective surfaces, as they were for Estes, for turning general vision into a 360-degree perspective. "You can either look through the window," Eddy said at the time, "or at the window, or at the reflection in the window. Nobody ever looks at all three at once, because it is impossible to focus on all three."[12]

The meticulous realism of Sylvia Plimack Mangold's *Floor with Light at 10:30 A.M.* of 1972 (page 47) belies its conceptual underpinnings, which are based on both perspective and the window image. Mangold rendered the view of her wooden floor according to Alberti. The apparent subject is light falling on the floor, controlled by the geometry of the actual window through which it passes. The exactitude of Mangold's painting and   25 precise reference to time masks a Duchampian connection. Light in window form is an apparition, to use Duchamp's phrase, of the real window in Mangold's studio, which does not appear in the painting. Cause and effect are separated in the picture's illusionistic space. On another level, Mangold reversed Alberti's dictum and projected an open window onto the painting itself to question the essential paradox of illusion and reality. On still another level, she equated the grid of her real window with the grid Alberti and Dürer (illus. 1) used to construct the illusion of space in painting. The convergence of grids—one actual, one conceptual—in Mangold's view of a corner of her studio at 10:30 A.M. ironically demonstrates the impossibility of capturing a fleeting moment of time through the painter's artifice.

The iconoclastic work of William T. Wiley wholeheartedly embraces both the perspectival window and window image and tells us about his singular personal vision. For a number of years Wiley has allied his quirky version of the boxlike space of Alberti's imaginary window with images of windows that recall fifteenth-century Flemish painting. Filled with symbols and surrounded by words, Wiley's windowed chambers are allegories for his life in the studio. In *The Prisoner Concept* of 1977 (page 64), for instance, the cell-like chamber suggests a locked-in view of reality molded by artistic conventions. The light coming through a solitary barred window in the far end of the chamber casts an impossible shadow on the left wall, reminding us that in the artist's alchemy, anything is possible. Like a magician, Wiley with his imagination has freed us to see the world anew.

Illus. 18. (Detail) EDWARD HOPPER, *Night Windows*, 1928, oil on canvas, 29 × 34 inches (73.6 × 86.3 cms). The Museum of Modern Art, New York, Gift of John Hay Whitney

Despite differences in style and sensibility, Wiley's seemingly naive works are as deceptive as the exacting realism of Sylvia Mangold's. His art contains elements of Duchamp's game of high seriousness. Like Duchamp's windows, Wiley's belong to a universe of his own in which the ambiguous nature of illusion and reality or apparition and appearance, as Duchamp called them, is continually reexamined. The multilayered window that commands *I Visit Bob* of 1981 (page 64) demonstrates the window's mutable nature in a drawing conceived in perspective, in the sparse geometry of constructivism, and in the gestural field of Abstract Expressionism. In short, it is a history of artistic conventions. In a more personal vein, the painting charts Wiley's course as an artist starting out in the late fifties in the full bloom of Abstract Expressionism. The

window's metamorphosis is witnessed by Big Eye, an anthropomorphic hybrid of Odilon Redon's all-seeing eye and Duchamp's eye charts. A now phallic Big Eye makes another appearance in three-dimensional form in the sculpture *Light Touches, Fall Colors* from 1982 (page 103), contemplating a winged window that calls up the window's long association with the female sex. Through these paired objects, reminiscent of the bride and the bachelors in Duchamp's *The Large Glass*, Wiley not only suggests the distinctions between painting and sculpture, but intimates an almost erotic exchange between observer and object, eye and mind.

The window, both ordinary object and metaphor, has been especially attractive since the early seventies to painters who have sought to move between abstraction and figuration and to imbue their painting with feeling. Howard Hodgkin acknowledged his admiration for Bonnard and Vuillard in his use of the window as both an image and a device for spatial illusion in *Lunch* of 1970–72 (page 37). He transformed Vuillard's richly patterned domestic interiors into a particularized, erotic atmosphere pulsating with vivid color and pointillist dots. Part striped, part black, Hodgkin's window seems to shift above the bright orange plane of the abstracted dining table. A wooden frame painted with brilliant orange and green stripes, like the window within, surrounds the inner wooden panel in relief. The frame is a deceit. Adopting the example of modernism and impressed by the inversions of European pictorial conventions in Indian miniatures, Hodgkin used the frame not to define a perspectival space according to Alberti, but to affirm the work of art as an object with a flat picture plane and, in another sense, to frame a visual equivalent of a singular past experience remembered.

By contrast, the window in John Walker's *Numinous*, a series which he began in 1977, is monumental. Walker was inspired by his own balcony window and its associations with similar windows in the history of art, notably the one in Matisse's *Piano Lesson* of 1916 (illus. 12) and in *The Balcony* of 1868 by Manet, who in turn was inspired by Goya. Architectural in scale, the window that opens out onto a balcony in *Numinous VII* of 1978 (page 91) gives the abstract forms behind the curving grill an ambivalent human quality. The window's decorative grill is a visual homage, as it has been for numerous others, to the French modernists and to the grand tradition of paintings which Walker has clearly embraced. Although the mingling of references to art's history intrigued both Walker and Hodgkin, their allusion to past masters carries none of Lichtenstein's irony. Rather, they draw sustenance from the windows of artists with whom they feel an affinity in order to enrich their own efforts to combine illusionistic spaces and images with the flat surfaces of abstraction.

Because a window is both flat and dimensional, it has become a natural subject in the seventies and eighties for a growing number of artists who wanted to fuse painting and sculptural object. Using stretchers that are architectural in presence and paint thickened with molding paste, Ralph Humphrey muscled his wall-abiding minimal canvases from the 1960s into the actual space of the room. The once windowlike recesses of a somber, monochromatic work like his *Untitled* of 1974 (page 77) burst forth into brilliantly colored, unabashed, and often folksy images of windows, replete with all the accessories associated with Pop Art—curtains, blinds, and windowsills. The near cuteness of the window in such works as *White Planes* of 1981–82 (page 94) is Humphrey's way of countering the sophistication of his aesthetic. The windblown curtain is meant not to heighten the drama of the scene as it does in Hopper's *Night Windows* (page 75, illus. 18), but to explore typical themes in American art. Humphrey's window image is ultimately a grid, his curtain a diagonal laid out with constructivist precision and enlivened by his well-tuned wit.

The *Window* and *Atmosphere* series Neil Jenney began in the early seventies and continues to investigate are poised on the tension between art as an object and as an illusion. Jenney's use of the frame, an architectural support essential to the spatial fiction of Renaissance art, was part of the determination of the artist and many contemporaries to counter the formalist requirement for pictorial flatness. To Jenney this was returning to realism. According to him: "Realism is illusionism and all illusionistic painting requires frames. I realized the frames would enhance the illusion and be a perfect place for the title."[13] Jenney's finely crafted frames with substantial moldings and edges painted in trompe l'oeil evoke such masterpieces of the past as the fifteenth-century portrait by Petrus Christus (illus. 5) and nineteenth-century American landscape paintings. Unlike the frame in Renaissance art which separates the painter's illusion from reality, Jenney's frame is an integral part of the form and content of *Atmo-*

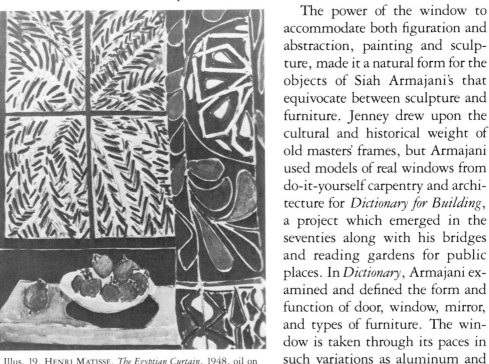

Illus. 19. HENRI MATISSE, *The Egyptian Curtain*, 1948, oil on canvas, 45¾ × 35 inches (116.2 × 88.9 cms). The Phillips Collection, Washington, DC

sphere of 1985 (page 67). The sheer physicality of the frame turns the work into an object suspended midway between painting and sculpture, art and reality. Its monumentality makes the clear blue expanse behind it deeper. The prominent windowsill carries the inscription ATMOSPHERE, expanding the meaning of the painting with language as Duchamp and Magritte had done in the first part of the century. The heavy frame and bold lettering capture our attention. The word ATMOSPHERE ensures that we will see the blue expanse as sky and, in turn, associate this painting with nineteenth-century landscape painting. Jenney's associations are emblematic of his desire to create works of art that focus on such a recurrent social issue as late-twentieth-century man's relation to the natural environment.

The power of the window to accommodate both figuration and abstraction, painting and sculpture, made it a natural form for the objects of Siah Armajani's that equivocate between sculpture and furniture. Jenney drew upon the cultural and historical weight of old masters' frames, but Armajani used models of real windows from do-it-yourself carpentry and architecture for *Dictionary for Building*, a project which emerged in the seventies along with his bridges and reading gardens for public places. In *Dictionary*, Armajani examined and defined the form and function of door, window, mirror, and types of furniture. The window is taken through its paces in such variations as aluminum and redwood windows, basement and ground-floor windows, and windows within windows. There are permutations of the window and door; *Door in Window #1* of 1979–82 (page 30), made of bronze screening and black wood, is the first. It appears to be a simple enough object. Yet, on closer scrutiny, its hidden oval form announces an eighteenth-century Jeffersonian model. This kind of layering of cultural history and visual message makes the window a compelling image to Armajani and other postmodernist artists. From a functional point of view, *Door in Window* questions the similarities and differences between two architectural types. How do windows and doors divide space? How does each function? By describing such conditions as open and closed, inside and outside, physical and psychological passage, *Door in Window* glides quietly from the world of tangible object into the realm of metaphysics. It is part of a complex system of artifice which, like its maker, is both forthright and elusive. In *Door in Window*, Armajani brought his sympathy for the social   27 dimension of public art to the individual viewer's private space. He has engaged us with mazelike structures that function like ordinary windows on a number of levels of meaning: practical object, architectural record, archetype, tangible embodiment of philosophical speculation.

In *A Short History of Modernist Painting* of 1982 (page 31) Mark Tansey presented an epic-sized allegory about the changing conventions governing pictorial representation, from Manet's time to the present, and offered an overview of the window in twentieth-century art. On the left the woman washing the combination windows with a garden hose stands for late nineteenth-century French painting, when the first modernist replaced the illusionistic trappings of Renaissance perspective and brought the Romantics' window image back to take its place as a spatial device. Ever the good narrator, Tansey backed up his story line with a correct period setting. The sharp contrast of light and dark colors suggests the flattened space the modernists discovered as well as the photographic surface that contributed to revolutionary reconsideration of the window view of Renaissance art. In the central episode of the allegory, a man futilely hits his head against a concrete wall standing in a wide open field. In both form and content this chapter illustrates not only the Abstract Expressionists' hard-headed quest for flat paintings with human significance, but the development of the modernist ambition by the single-minded formalist painters of the sixties. The third scene is set in the softly lit corner of a room rendered in Renaissance perspective. Here a hen perched on an uplifting ramp gazes at its own reflection in an appropriately framed mirror. The episode brings Tansey's ironic postmodern epic up to the eighties and the return of spatial illusion, the recognizable image, the frame of Renaissance art, and the illusionistic enterprise of the present.

The windows in Catherine Murphy's paintings are conceived with the full understanding of the history of modernist painting, and convey delight in the world seen and

known through an observant eye, rather than the ironic tone of Tansey's epic allegory. Both abstract and real windows suit Murphy's intent to paint representations of the perceived world. In *Nighttime Self-Portrait* of 1985 (page 7) the cross-supports of an ordinary window, down to the ragged stretch of paint on the windowpane where the house painter missed the mark, divide the canvas into horizontal and vertical planes with the rigor of Mondrian. In *Self-Portraits* of 1985 (page 38), a view of the artist and her model, the sculptor Harry Roseman, her husband, the traditional genders of the artist and the model have been reversed. Gone are the voluptuous female nudes of Dürer and Matisse. The window, the wall, the mirror—all surrogates for the painter's canvas—are shown and contribute to the spatial illusions. Underneath the painting's specificity, which is exact to the meticulously painted blue flocked wallpaper, Murphy challenged the realist tradition and the grand theme of the artist's studio. Heralded by Velázquez in *Las Meninas* at the end of the seventeenth century, established in the mid-nineteenth century by Courbet, and extended by Matisse (illus. 9) and Picasso (page 85), the theme of the artist's studio celebrates the privileged space where an empty canvas becomes a window that opens the artist's imagination to the viewer.

In the creation of their new views, artists in our century have transformed the ancient symbol of the window and made it unabashedly a form and subject of art. They have stretched the window's geometry into hitherto unimagined spaces and freedoms of color. In so doing they have offered for our contemplation their own visions, from poetic to ironic, enabling us to mediate between the past and the present to see the world anew. Artists have expanded the window image with new layers of form and meaning that make us, not passive onlookers, but active participants in the creative process. And they have enriched art's history with such power of imagination that we are assured the human eye remains the window of the soul.

N O T E S

1. Henri Matisse quoted in Pierre Schneider, *Matisse* (New York 1984), p. 45.
2. Leon Battista Alberti, *On Painting and On Sculpture: The Latin Texts of "De Pittura" and "De Statua,"* trans. Cecil Grayson (London 1972), 1:19, p. 55.
3. See Lorenz Eitner, "The Open Window and the Storm Tossed Boat," *Art Bulletin*, 37, December 1955, pp. 281–90.
4. See Aaron Scharf, *Art and Photography* (New York 1968).
5. Maurice Denis quoted in Herschel B. Chipp, ed. *Theories of Modern Art: A Source by Artists and Critics* (Berkeley and Los Angeles 1968), p. 106.
6. Henri Matisse quoted in Schneider, p. 464.
7. René Magritte quoted in Suzi Gablik, *Magritte* (Greenwich, CT 1970), p. 182.
8. Adolph Gottlieb quoted in *Adolph Gottlieb. A Retrospective*. Text by Lawrence Alloway and Mary Davis MacNaughton (New York 1981), p. 4.
9. This suggestion was made by Bonnie Clearwater, then Director of The Mark Rothko Foundation, New York, in a conversation in the fall of 1984.
10. Hans Hofmann quoted in *Hans Hofmann*, introduction by Sam Hunter (New York 1963), p. 46.
11. Ellsworth Kelly quoted in John Coplans, *Ellsworth Kelly* (New York n.d.), p. 28.
12. Don Eddy quoted in John Hallmark Neff, "Painting and Perception: Don Eddy," *Arts Magazine*, 54, December 1979, pp. 98–102.
13. Neil Jenney quoted in *New Image Painting*. Essay by Richard Marshall (New York 1978), p. 38.

You will lift the curtain
And now look at the window opening
Spiders when hands wove the light
Beauty paleness unfathomable violet tints

O Paris
The yellow fades from red to green
Paris Vancouver Hyères Maintenon New York and the Antilles
The window opens like an orange
Lovely fruit of light

GUILLAUME APOLLINAIRE
"Windows" 1918

SIAH ARMAJANI
Dictionary for Building:
Door in Window #1 1979–82
Stedelijk Museum

MARK TANSEY
A Short History of Modernist Painting 1982
Collection Martin Sklar

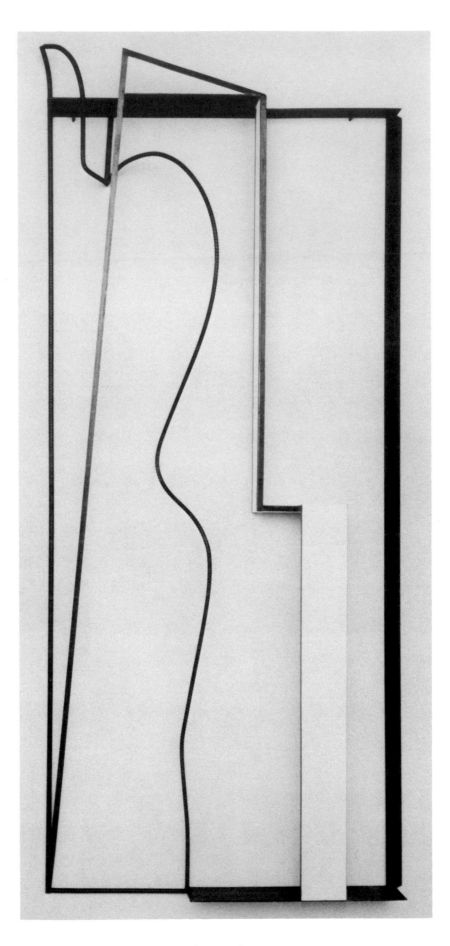

BRYAN HUNT
Corridor 1983
Collection Warner Communications Inc.
Courtesy Blum Helman Gallery

ROBERT DELAUNAY
Les Fenêtres (Windows) 1912
Collection Charles Altshul

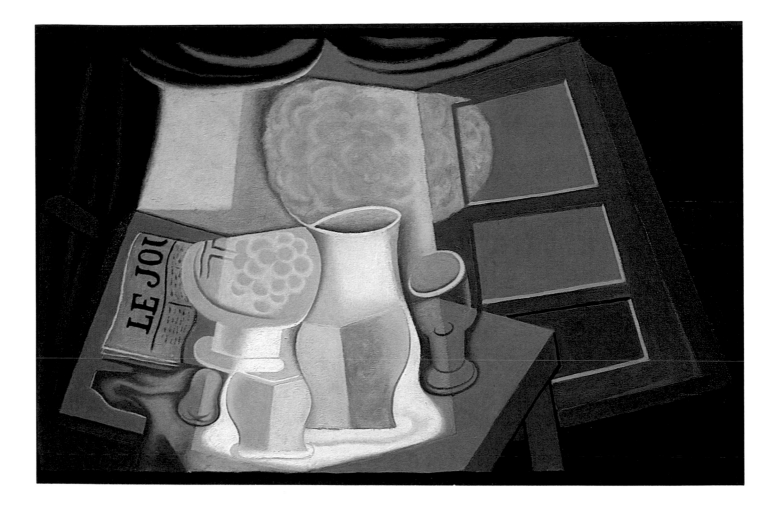

Above:
Juan Gris
The Table in Front of the Window 1921
Collection Dr. and Mrs. Raymond Sackler

Left:
Marc Chagall
Dream Village 1929
McNay Art Museum
Bequest of Marion Koogler McNay

EDOUARD VUILLARD
At the Window circa 1900
Collection Mrs. Wellington Henderson

HOWARD HODGKIN
Lunch 1970–72
Collection Friends of the Neuberger Museum
State University of New York at Purchase

CATHERINE MURPHY
Self-Portraits 1985
Private collection

Courtesy Xavier Fourcade, Inc.

RAOUL DUFY
Open Window, Nice 1928
The Art Institute of Chicago
The Joseph Winterbotham Collection

ROBERT MOTHERWELL
The Garden Window (formerly Open No. 110) Summer 1969
Collection the artist

ROBERT MOTHERWELL
Spanish Picture with Window 1941
Collection the artist

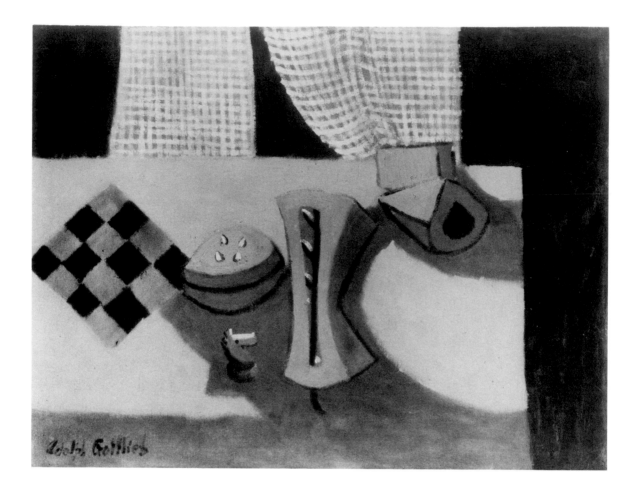

Above:
ADOLPH GOTTLIEB
Untitled (Pink Still Life—Curtains and Gourds) 1938
© Adolph and Esther Gottlieb
Foundation, Inc.

Right:
ADOLPH GOTTLIEB
Evil Omen 1946
Neuberger Museum
State University of New York at Purchase
Gift of Roy R. Neuberger

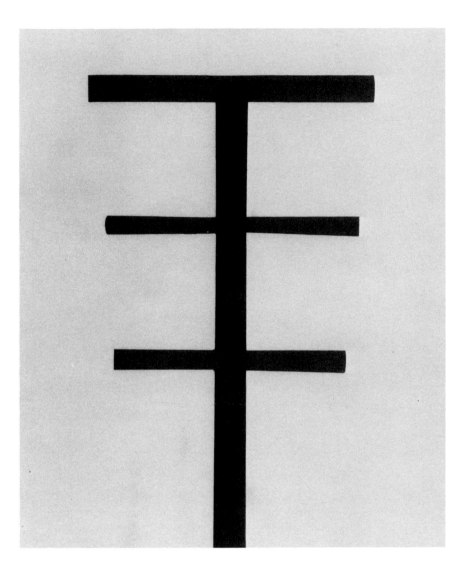

Above:
ELLSWORTH KELLY
Window I 1949
Collection the artist

Left:
ELLSWORTH KELLY
Window, Museum of Modern Art, Paris 1949
Collection the artist

Right:
ELLSWORTH KELLY
Window V 1950
Collection the artist

ELLSWORTH KELLY
Black and White (Carpenter's Window) 1955
Collection the artist

46

SYLVIA PLIMACK MANGOLD
Floor with Light at 10:30 A.M. 1972
Oliver–Hoffmann Collection

FAIRFIELD PORTER
Anne in a Striped Dress 1967
The Parrish Art Museum
Gift of the Estate of Fairfield Porter

JANE FREILICHER
Flowers Gathered in September 1978
Private collection, USA

Above:
Tom Wesselmann
Great American Nude #35 1962
Virginia Museum of Fine Arts
Gift of Sydney and Frances Lewis

Right:
Edward Kienholz and
Nancy Reddin Kienholz
Deep Purple Rage 1981
L.A. Louver Gallery

RENÉ MAGRITTE
La chambre d'écoute (The Listening Room) 1953
Private collection, California

RENÉ MAGRITTE
La clef des songes (The Key of Dreams) 1936
Collection Jasper Johns

SHIGEKO KUBOTA
Meta-Marcel Window 1976
Collection the artist

PETE OMLOR
Untitled (Window) 1978
Collection The Chase Manhattan Bank, N.A.

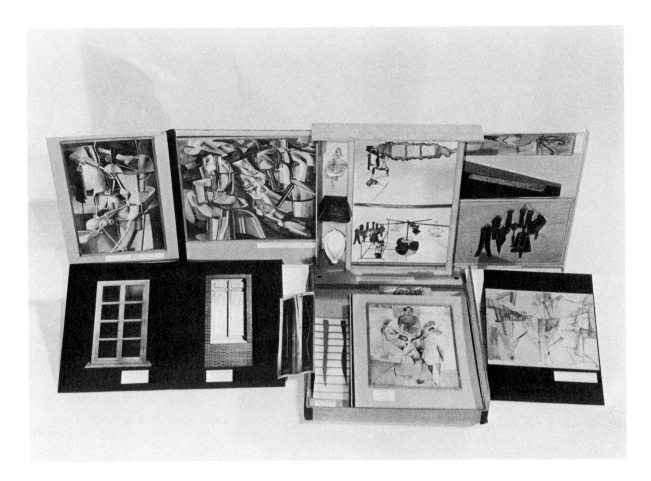

Above:
MARCEL DUCHAMP
Boîte–en–Valise (Box in a Valise) 1941
Oklahoma Art Center
Washington Gallery of Modern Art Collection

Left:
MARCEL DUCHAMP
Photographic reproduction of Marcel Duchamp's
La Mariée mise à nu par ses célibataires,
même (le Grand Verre); The Bride Stripped Bare
by Her Bachelors, Even (The Large Glass)
1973 after original of 1915–23
The Museum of Modern Art, New York
Fabricated by and gift of the GAF Corporation

RICHARD ARTSCHWAGER
Untitled 1966
Cincinnati Art Museum
Gift of RSM Co.

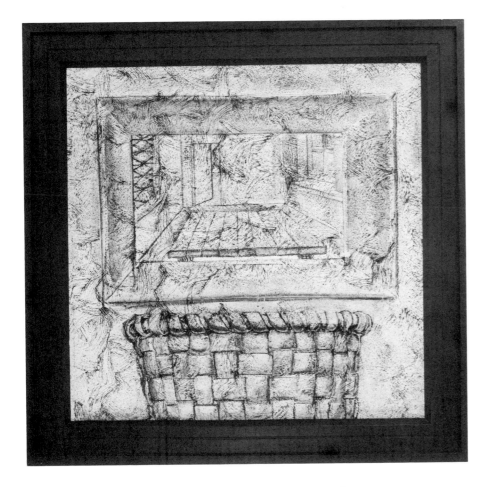

Above:
RICHARD ARTSCHWAGER
Window to the Right #2 1977
Collection Mr. and Mrs. James Harithas

Left:
RICHARD ARTSCHWAGER
Upper Right Hand Window 1986
Leo Castelli Gallery

Top left:
EVA HESSE
Untitled 1969
Collection Agnes Gund

Top right:
EVA HESSE
Untitled 1968
Collection Sondra G. Gilman

Bottom left:
EVA HESSE
Untitled 1969
Private collection

Bottom right:
EVA HESSE
Untitled 1968
Neuberger Museum
State University of
New York at Purchase
Gift of Roy R. Neuberger

Above:
RICHARD ESTES
Diner 1971
Hirshhorn Museum and Sculpture Garden
Smithsonian Institution

Right:
DON EDDY
New Shoes 1973
Williams College Museum of Art

Above:
WILLIAM T. WILEY
I Visit Bob 1981
Collection Martin Sklar

Right:
WILLIAM T. WILEY
The Prisoner Concept 1977
The Morgan Gallery

WILLIAM T. WILEY
Scam Quentin 1981
Collection Mr. and Mrs. William C. Janss

ROY LICHTENSTEIN
Paintings Near Window 1983
Collection Shirley and Miles Fiterman

NEIL JENNEY
Atmosphere 1985
Collection the artist

DAVID HOCKNEY
Henry Geldzahler and Christopher Scott 1968–69
Robert E. Abrams Family Collection

BALTHUS
The Window 1933
Indiana University Art Museum

RENÉ MAGRITTE
Le soir qui tombe (Evening Falls) 1964
Private collection

EDWARD HOPPER
The Barber Shop 1931
Neuberger Museum
State University of New York at Purchase
Gift of Roy R. Neuberger

RICHARD DIEBENKORN
Woman in a Window 1957
Albright–Knox Art Gallery
Gift of Seymour H. Knox

RICHARD DIEBENKORN
Ocean Park #111 1978
Hirshhorn Museum and Sculpture Garden
Smithsonian Institution

73

EDWARD HOPPER
Morning Sun 1952
Columbus Museum of Art
Museum purchase, Howald Fund

EDWARD HOPPER
Night Windows 1928
The Museum of Modern Art, New York
Gift of John Hay Whitney

ROBERT BERLIND
Lightspill II 1980
Collection the artist

RALPH HUMPHREY
Untitled 1974
Collection Lannan Foundation

JOSEPH CORNELL
Untitled (Window box construction) n.d.
Estate of Joseph Cornell
Courtesy The Pace Gallery

JOSEPH CORNELL
Observatory Columba Carrousel circa 1953
Estate of Joseph Cornell
Courtesy The Pace Gallery

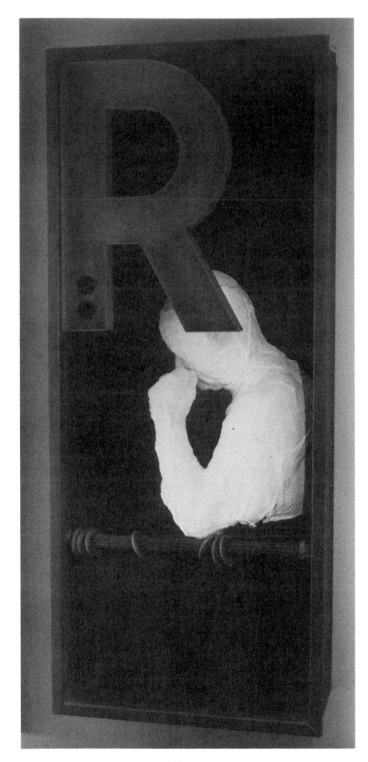

Above:
GEORGE SEGAL
Box: Man in a Bar 1969
Museum of Contemporary Art, Chicago
Gift of Mr. and Mrs. E. A. Bergman

Right:
GEORGE SEGAL
Girl Sitting against a Wall II 1970
Akron Art Museum
Purchased with the aid of funds
from the 50th Anniversary Gala

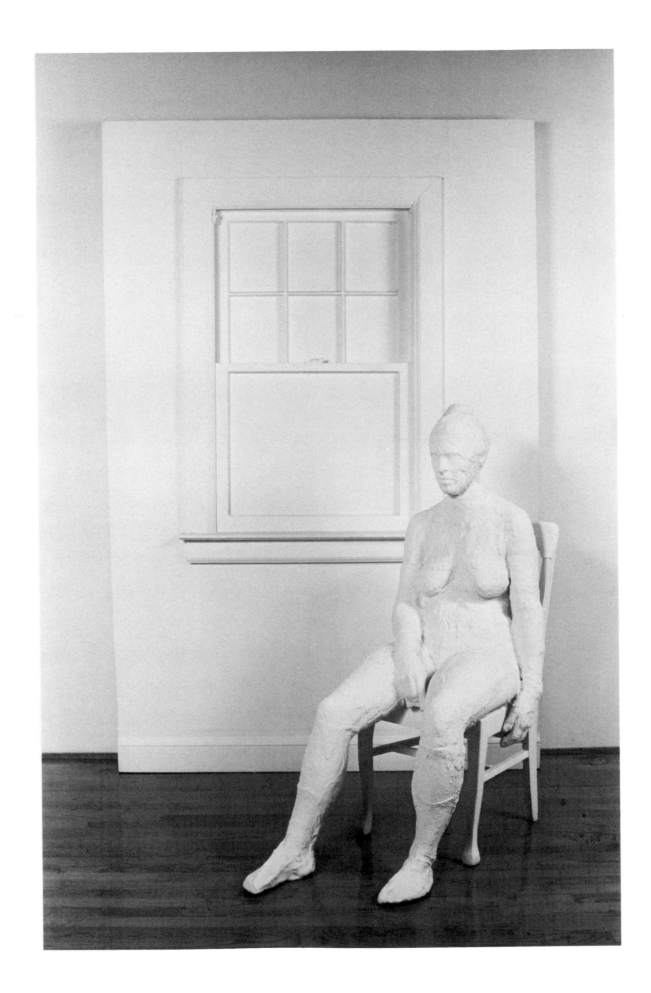

ROY LICHTENSTEIN
Curtains 1962
Jointly owned by The Saint Louis Art Museum
and Mr. and Mrs. Joseph Pulitzer, Jr.

ROY LICHTENSTEIN
Stretcher Frame with Cross Bars II 1968
Collection Mr. and Mrs. Leo Castelli

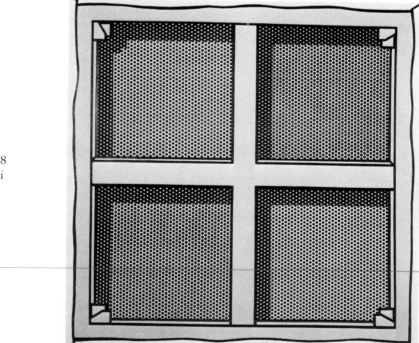

ROY LICHTENSTEIN
Still Life with Folded Sheets 1976
Virginia Museum of Fine Arts
Gift of The Sydney and
Frances Lewis Foundation

Above:
PABLO PICASSO
Studio in a Painted Frame 2 April 1956
The Museum of Modern Art, New York
Gift of Mr. and Mrs. Werner E. Josten

Left:
MARSDEN HARTLEY
Sea Window, Tinker Mackerel 1942
Smith College Museum of Art

RAOUL DUFY
The Artist's Studio 1935
The Phillips Collection

HANS HOFMANN
Untitled 1941
André Emmerich Gallery

HANS HOFMANN
Untitled 1942
André Emmerich Gallery

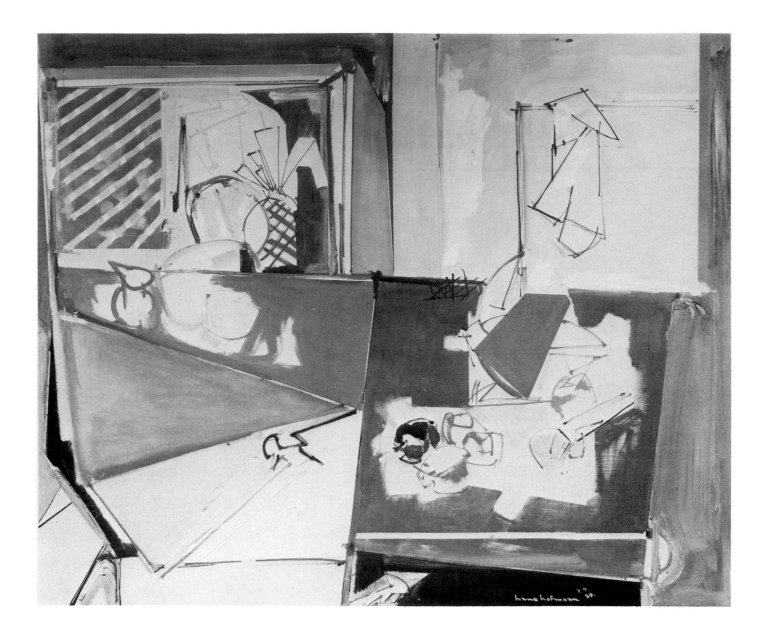

Above:
HANS HOFMANN
Magenta and Blue 1950
Whitney Museum of American Art

Right:
HANS HOFMANN
Auxerre, France. St. Etienne's
Glorious Light Emanated
by Its Windows, as Remembered 1960
Collection Mrs. Robert B. Eichholz

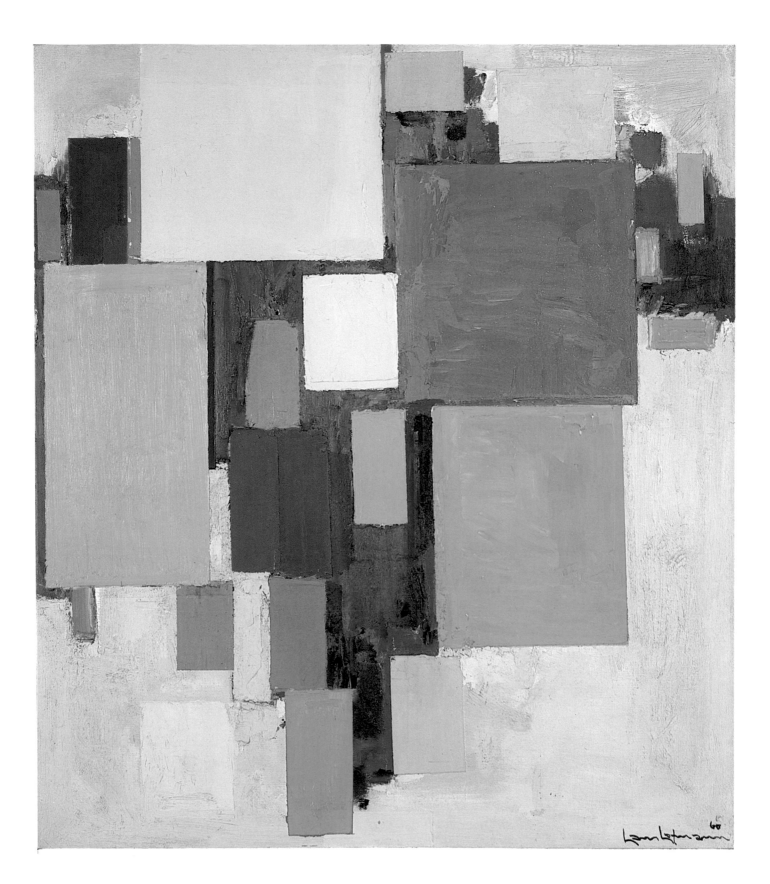

89

CHRISTO
Yellow Store Front 1965
Collection Holly and Horace Solomon

JOHN WALKER
Numinous VII 1978
The Edward R. Broida Trust

Above:
JASPER JOHNS
Studio 2 1966
Collection Mr. and Mrs. Victor W. Ganz

Left:
MILTON AVERY
Seated Girl with Dog 1944
Collection Roy R. Neuberger

RALPH HUMPHREY
White Planes 1981–82
Private collection, Washington, DC

GENE DAVIS
Blue Rectangle I 1957
Collection Mr. and Mrs. I. Irving Feldman

MARK ROTHKO
Old Gold over White 1956
Neuberger Museum
State University of New York at Purchase
Gift of Roy R. Neuberger

MARK ROTHKO
Untitled
(Two Women at the Window)
late 1930s
National Gallery of Art,
Washington
Gift of The Mark Rothko
Foundation

MARK ROTHKO
Untitled 1941–43
Neuberger Museum
State University of New York
at Purchase
Gift of The Mark Rothko
Foundation

ROBERT MOSKOWITZ
Untitled 1962
Collection·the artist

LOOKING from outside into an open window one never sees as much as when one looks through a closed window. There is nothing more profound, more mysterious, more pregnant, more insidious, more dazzling than a window lighted by a single candle. What one can see out in the sunlight is always less interesting than what goes on behind a window pane. In that black or luminous square life lives, life dreams, life suffers.

CHARLES BAUDELAIRE
"Windows" 1864

CATALOGUE TO THE EXHIBITION

*Dimensions are given in inches followed by
centimeters: height precedes length precedes depth.
All works will be shown in Purchase and
Houston unless otherwise indicated.*

SIAH ARMAJANI
American, born Iran 1939–

Dictionary for Building: Door in Window #1
1979–82
painted wood, bronze screen, and
plexiglass
104 × 48 × 22 inches (264.1 × 121.9
× 55.9 cms)
Stedelijk Museum
(Only at Purchase)

RICHARD ARTSCHWAGER
American 1923–

Untitled 1966
formica on wood
24 × 36 × 5 inches (60.9 × 91.4
× 12.7 cms)
Cincinnati Art Museum
Gift of RSM Co.

Window to the Right #2 1977
ink on paper
23¾ × 35 inches (60.3 × 88.9 cms)
Collection Mr. and Mrs. James Harithas

Upper Right Hand Window 1986
painted wood and celotex
51 × 51 × 2½ inches (129.5 × 129.5
× 6.3 cms)
Leo Castelli Gallery

MILTON AVERY
American 1885–1965

Seated Girl with Dog 1944
oil on canvas
44 × 32 inches (111.7 × 81.3 cms)
Collection Roy R. Neuberger

BALTHUS
French 1908–

The Window 1933
oil on canvas
63¼ × 44⅛ inches (160.6 × 112.2 cms)
Indiana University Art Museum

ROBERT BERLIND
American 1938–

Lightspill II 1980
oil on canvas
68 × 76 inches (172.7 × 193 cms)
Collection the artist

MARC CHAGALL
French, born Russia 1887–1985

Dream Village 1929
oil on canvas
46½ × 36½ inches (118.1 × 92.7 cms)
McNay Art Museum
Bequest of Marion Koogler McNay

CHRISTO
American, born Bulgaria 1935–

Yellow Store Front 1965
wood, plexiglass, fabric, brown paper,
galvanized metal, pegboard, and electric
light
98 × 88¼ × 16 inches (248.9 × 224.1
× 40.6 cms)
Collection Holly and Horace Solomon

JOSEPH CORNELL
American 1903–72

Observatory Columba Carrousel circa 1953
wood, glass, mirror, metal, paper
18¹/₁₆ × 11⁹/₁₆ × 5¹³/₁₆ inches (45.9
× 29.2 × 15.1 cms)
Estate of Joseph Cornell
Courtesy The Pace Gallery

Untitled (Window box construction) n.d.
wood, glass, mirror
18 × 11 × 5¾ inches (45.7 × 27.9
× 14.6 cms)
Estate of Joseph Cornell
Courtesy The Pace Gallery

GENE DAVIS
American 1920–85

Blue Rectangle I 1957
oil on raw canvas
93 × 80 inches (236.2 × 203.2 cms)
Collection Mr. and Mrs. I. Irving Feldman

ROBERT DELAUNAY
French 1885–1941

Les Fenêtres (Windows) 1912
oil on canvas
18 × 15 inches (45.7 × 38.1 cms)
Collection Charles Altschul
(Only at Purchase)

RICHARD DIEBENKORN
American 1922–

Woman in a Window 1957
oil on canvas
59 × 56 inches (149.9 × 142.2 cms)
Albright–Knox Art Gallery
Gift of Seymour H. Knox

Ocean Park #111 1978
oil and charcoal on canvas
93⅛ × 93¼ inches (236.5 × 236.8 cms)
Hirshhorn Museum and Sculpture Garden,
Smithsonian Institution

MARCEL DUCHAMP
American, born France 1887–1968

Photographic reproduction of Marcel
Duchamp's *La Mariée mise à nu par ses
célibataires, même (le Grand Verre); The Bride
Stripped Bare by Her Bachelors, Even (The
Large Glass)*
1973 after original of 1915–23
photographic transparencies, glass, and
aluminum
115¼ × 70⅞ × 4⅛ inches (292.7
× 180 × 10.4 cms)
The Museum of Modern Art, New York
Fabricated by and gift of the GAF
Corporation

Fresh Widow 1920 (third version 1964)
miniature French window, painted wood
frame, and eight panes of glass covered
with black leather
30½ × 20⅞ × 3⁵/₁₆ inches (77.4 × 53
× 8.4 cms)
edition of eight signed and numbered
replicas
published by Galleria Schwarz, Milan
Indiana University Art Museum
Partial gift of Mrs. William Conroy

Boîte–en–Valise (Box in a Valise) 1941
boxed set of reproduced objects, drawings,
paintings, and prints
16 × 14⅝ × 3½ inches (40.6 × 37.1
× 8.8 cms)
regular edition not to exceed 300
Oklahoma Art Center
Permanent Collection
Washington Gallery of Modern Art
Collection

RAOUL DUFY
French 1877–1953

Open Window, Nice 1928
oil on canvas
25¾ × 21⅜ inches (65.4 × 54.3 cms)
The Art Institute of Chicago
The Joseph Winterbotham Collection

The Artist's Studio 1935
oil on canvas
46¾ × 58¼ inches (119 × 148 cms)
The Phillips Collection
(Only at Purchase)

DON EDDY
American 1944–

New Shoes 1973
acrylic on canvas
54 × 48 inches (137.2 × 121.9 cms)
Williams College Museum of Art

RICHARD ESTES
American 1936–

Diner 1971
oil on canvas
45 × 55⅛ × 4⅛ inches (114.3 × 140
× 10.5 cms)
Hirshhorn Museum and Sculpture Garden,
Smithsonian Institution

JANE FREILICHER
American 1924–

Flowers Gathered in September 1978
oil on canvas
60 × 50 inches (152.4 × 127 cms)
Private collection, USA

ADOLPH GOTTLIEB
American 1903–74

*Untitled (Pink Still Life—Curtains and
Gourds)* 1938
oil on canvas
30 × 39¾ inches (76.2 × 100.9 cms)
© 1981 Adolph and Esther Gottlieb
Foundation, Inc.

Evil Omen 1946
oil on canvas
38 × 30 inches (96.5 × 76.2 cms)
Neuberger Museum, State University of
New York at Purchase
Gift of Roy R. Neuberger

JUAN GRIS
Spanish 1887–1927

The Table in Front of the Window 1921
oil on canvas
25⅝ × 39½ inches (65 × 100.3 cms)
Collection Dr. and Mrs. Raymond Sackler
(Only at Purchase)

MARSDEN HARTLEY
American 1877–1943

Sea Window, Tinker Mackerel 1942
oil on canvas
40 × 30 inches (101.6 × 76.2 cms)
Smith College Museum of Art

EVA HESSE
American, born Germany 1936–70

Untitled 1968
ink with wash on paper
11 × 15 inches (27.9 × 38.1 cms)
Neuberger Museum, State University of
New York at Purchase
Gift of Roy R. Neuberger

Untitled 1968
ink with wash on paper
13 × 13 inches (33 × 33 cms)
Collection Sondra G. Gilman

Untitled 1969
gouache, watercolor,
silver and bronze paint on paper
30⅛ × 25¼ inches (76.5 × 64.1 cms)
Collection Agnes Gund

Untitled 1969
pencil and gouache on paper
22½ × 16½ inches (57.1 × 41.9 cms)
Private collection

DAVID HOCKNEY
British 1937–

Henry Geldzahler and Christopher Scott
1968–69
acrylic on canvas
84 × 120 inches (213.3 × 304.8 cms)
Robert E. Abrams Family Collection
(Only at Purchase)

HOWARD HODGKIN
British 1937–

Lunch 1970–72
oil on wood
33 × 36 inches (83.8 × 91.4 cms)
Collection Friends of the Neuberger
Museum, State University of New York at
Purchase

HANS HOFMANN
American, born Germany 1880–1966

Untitled 1941
crayon and ink on paper
17 × 14 inches (43.2 × 35.5 cms)
André Emmerich Gallery

Untitled 1942
crayon and ink on paper
14 × 17 inches (35.5 × 43.2 cms)
André Emmerich Gallery

Magenta and Blue 1950
oil on canvas
47½ × 57¾ inches (120.6 × 146.7 cms)
Whitney Museum of American Art

*Auxerre, France. St. Etienne's Glorious Light
Emanated by Its Windows, as Remembered*
1960
oil on canvas
60 × 52 inches (152.4 × 132 cms)
Collection Mrs. Robert B. Eichholz

EDWARD HOPPER
American 1882–1967

Night Windows 1928
oil on canvas
29 × 34 inches (73.6 × 86.3 cms)
The Museum of Modern Art, New York
Gift of John Hay Whitney

The Barber Shop 1931
oil on canvas
60 × 78 inches (152.4 × 198.1 cms)
Neuberger Museum, State University of
New York at Purchase
Gift of Roy R. Neuberger

Morning Sun 1952
oil on canvas
36½ × 48⅜ inches (92.7 × 122.8 cms)
Columbus Museum of Art
Museum purchase, Howald Fund
(Only at Purchase)

RALPH HUMPHREY
American 1932–

Untitled 1974
acrylic on canvas
54 × 54 inches (137.1 × 137.1 cms)
Collection Lannan Foundation

White Planes 1981–82
acrylic and modeling paste on wood and
canvas
54 × 72½ inches (137.1 × 184.1 cms)
Private collection, Washington, DC

BRYAN HUNT
American 1947–

Corridor 1983
welded steel and spackling compound
144 × 64 × 11 inches (365.7
× 162.5 × 27.9 cms)
Collection Warner Communications Inc.
Courtesy Blum Helman Gallery

NEIL JENNEY
American 1945–

Atmosphere 1985
oil on wood
33¼ × 79½ × 5⅛ inches (84.4
× 201.9 × 13 cms)
Collection the artist

JASPER JOHNS
American 1930–

Studio 2 1966
oil on canvas
70 × 125 inches (177.8 × 317.5 cms)
Collection Mr. and Mrs. Victor W. Ganz
(Only at Purchase)

ELLSWORTH KELLY
American 1923–

Window, Museum of Modern Art, Paris 1949
oil on wood and canvas, two joined panels
60 × 30 × ¾ inches (152.4 × 76.2 × 1.9 cms)
Collection the artist
(Only at Purchase)

Window I 1949
oil on wood
34¾ × 30¼ inches (88.2 × 76.8 cms)
Collection the artist

Window V 1950
oil on wood
41 × 23¾ inches (104.1 × 60.3 cms)
Collection the artist

Black and White (Carpenter's Window) 1955
oil on canvas
69¼ × 39¼ inches (175.9 × 99.7 cms)
Collection the artist

EDWARD KIENHOLZ
AND NANCY REDDIN KIENHOLZ
Americans Edward 1927–
Nancy Reddin 1943–

Deep Purple Rage 1981
mixed media
60 × 48 × 30 inches (152.4 × 121.9 × 76.2 cms)
L. A. Louver Gallery

SHIGEKO KUBOTA
Japanese 1937–

Meta-Marcel Window 1976
glass, wood construction, TV set, playback deck, and videotape
18¼ × 12¼ × 3⅜ inches (46.3 × 31.1 × 8.5 cms)
Collection the artist

ROY LICHTENSTEIN
American 1923–

Stretcher Frame with Cross Bars II 1968
oil and magna on canvas
48 × 48 inches (121.9 × 121.9 cms)
Collection Mr. and Mrs. Leo Castelli
(Only at Purchase)

Curtains 1962
oil and magna on canvas
68 × 57¾ inches (172.7 × 146.6 cms)
Jointly owned by The Saint Louis Art Museum and Mr. and Mrs. Joseph Pulitzer, Jr.
(Only at Purchase)

Still Life with Folded Sheets 1976
oil and magna on canvas
70 × 50 inches (177.8 × 127 cms)
Virginia Museum of Fine Arts
Gift of The Sydney and Frances Lewis Foundation

Paintings Near Window 1983
oil and magna on canvas
50 × 60 inches (127 × 152.4 cms)
Collection Shirley and Miles Fiterman
(Only at Purchase)

RENÉ MAGRITTE
Belgian 1898–1967

La clef des songes (The Key of Dreams) 1936
oil on canvas
16¼ × 10¾ inches (41.3 × 27.3 cms)
Collection Jasper Johns
(Only at Purchase)

La chambre d'écoute (The Listening Room) 1953
oil on canvas
31 × 39⅜ inches (80 × 100 cms)
Private collection, California

Le soir qui tombe (Evening Falls) 1964
oil on canvas
63¾ × 51¼ inches (162 × 130.1 cms)
Private collection

SYLVIA PLIMACK MANGOLD
American 1938–

Floor with Light at 10:30 A.M. 1972
acrylic on canvas
52 × 61 inches (132.1 × 154.9 cms)
Oliver–Hoffmann Collection

HENRI MATISSE
French 1869–1954

The Green Pumpkin circa 1920
oil on canvas
30½ × 24½ inches (77.4 × 62.2 cms)
Museum of Art, Rhode Island School of Design
Anonymous gift

ROBERT MOSKOWITZ
American 1935–

Untitled 1962
oil and collage on canvas
80 × 54 inches (203.2 × 137.1 cms)
Collection the artist

ROBERT MOTHERWELL
American 1915–

Spanish Picture with Window 1941
oil on canvas
42 × 34 inches (106.7 × 86.3 cms)
Collection the artist

The Garden Window (formerly Open No. 110) Summer 1969
acrylic on sized canvas
61 × 41 inches (154.9 × 104.1 cms)
Collection the artist

CATHERINE MURPHY
American 1946–

Nighttime Self-Portrait 1985
oil on canvas
16¾ × 16⅛ inches (42.5 × 40.9 cms)
Collection Mrs. Robert M. Benjamin

Self-Portraits 1985
oil on canvas
38 × 45 inches (96.5 × 114.3 cms)
Private collection
Courtesy Xavier Fourcade, Inc.

PETE OMLOR
American 1947–

Untitled (Window) 1978
sugar pine, fiber glass, screen, and enamel
84 × 72 inches (213.3 × 182.9 cms)
Collection The Chase Manhattan Bank, N.A.

PABLO PICASSO
Spanish 1881–1973

Studio in a Painted Frame 2 April 1956
oil on canvas
35 × 45⅝ inches (88.9 × 115.9 cms)
The Museum of Modern Art, New York
Gift of Mr. and Mrs. Werner E. Josten

FAIRFIELD PORTER
American 1907–75

Anne in a Striped Dress 1967
oil on canvas
61¼ × 49½ inches (155.5 × 125.7 cms)
The Parrish Art Museum
Gift of the Estate of Fairfield Porter

MARK ROTHKO
American, born Latvia 1903–70

Untitled (Two Women at the Window) late 1930s
oil on canvas
36 × 24 inches (91.4 × 60.9 cms)
National Gallery of Art, Washington
Gift of The Mark Rothko Foundation

Untitled 1941–43
oil on canvas
32 × 23⅞ inches (81.3 × 60.6 cms)
Neuberger Museum, State University of New York at Purchase
Gift of The Mark Rothko Foundation

Old Gold over White 1956
oil on canvas
68 × 46 inches (172.7 × 116.8 cms)
Neuberger Museum, State University of New York at Purchase
Gift of Roy R. Neuberger

GEORGE SEGAL
American 1924–

Box: Man in a Bar 1969
plaster, wood, metal, and cloth
60½ × 24½ × 12⅜ inches
(153.6 × 62.2 × 31.4 cms)
Museum of Contemporary Art, Chicago
Gift of Mr. and Mrs. E. A. Bergman

Girl Sitting against a Wall II 1970
plaster, wood, glass
91 × 60 × 40 inches (231.1 × 152.4
× 101.6 cms)
Akron Art Museum
Purchased with the aid of funds from the
50th Anniversary Gala

MARK TANSEY
American 1949–

A Short History of Modernist Painting 1982
oil on canvas
58 × 120 inches (147.3 × 304.8 cms)
Collection Martin Sklar

EDOUARD VUILLARD
French 1868–1940

At the Window circa 1900
oil on canvas
19¼ × 24½ inches (48.9 × 62.2 cms)
Collection Mrs. Wellington Henderson
(Only at Purchase)

JOHN WALKER
British 1931–

Numinous VII 1978
oil and acrylic on canvas
120 × 96 inches (304.8 × 243.8 cms)
The Edward R. Broida Trust

TOM WESSELMANN
American 1931–

Great American Nude #35 1962
mixed media, construction with acrylic,
enamel, and collage on composition board
48 × 60 × 2 inches (121.9 × 152.4
× 5.1 cms)
Virginia Museum of Fine Arts
Gift of Sydney and Frances Lewis

WILLIAM T. WILEY
American 1937–

The Prisoner Concept 1977
graphite and wax on parchment
38 × 25⅛ inches (96.5 × 63.8 cms)
The Morgan Gallery

I Visit Bob 1981
acrylic and charcoal on canvas
44¼ × 47½ inches (112.4 × 120.6 cms)
Collection Martin Sklar

Scam Quentin 1981
watercolor on paper
22 × 30 inches (55.9 × 76.2 cms)
Collection Mr. and Mrs. William C. Janss

Light Touches, Fall Colors 1982
steel, aluminum, brass, and paint
55 × 52 × 25 inches (139.7 × 132.1
× 63.5 cms)
Collection the artist and Lippincott
Foundry

WILLIAM T. WILEY
Light Touches, Fall Colors 1982
Collection the artist
and Lippincott Foundry

Books

Arnason, H. H. *Robert Motherwell.* New York: Harry N. Abrams, Inc., 1977.

Ashton, Dore. *American Art since 1945.* New York: Oxford University Press, 1982.

Bourdon, David. *Christo.* New York: Harry N. Abrams, Inc., 1971.

Buckberrough, Sherry A. *Robert Delaunay: The Discovery of Simultaneity.* Ann Arbor, MI: UMI Research Press, 1982.

Cabanne, Pierre. *Dialogues with Marcel Duchamp.* Translated by Ron Pagett. New York: The Viking Press, 1971.

The Complete Works of Marcel Duchamp. Text by Arturo Schwarz. New York: Harry N. Abrams, Inc., 1969.

Coplans, John. *Ellsworth Kelly.* New York: Harry N. Abrams, Inc., n.d.

Coplans, John, ed. *Roy Lichtenstein.* New York: Praeger Inc., 1972.

Duchamp, Marcel. *Notes and Projects for the Large Glass by Marcel Duchamp.* Selected, ordered, and with an introduction by Arturo Schwarz. New York: Harry N. Abrams, Inc., 1969.

Flam, Jack D., ed. *Matisse on Art.* London: Phaidon, 1973.

Francis, Richard. *Jasper Johns.* New York: Abbeville Press, 1984.

Gablik, Suzi. *Magritte.* Greenwich, CT: New York Graphic Society, 1970.

————. *Progress in Art.* New York: Rizzoli International Publications, 1977.

Golding, John. *Marcel Duchamp: The Bride Stripped Bare by Her Bachelors, Even.* New York: The Viking Press, 1972.

Gombrich, E. H. *Art and Illusion: A Study in the Psychology of Pictorial Representation.* New York: Pantheon Books, 1960.

Goodrich, Lloyd. *Edward Hopper.* New York: Harry N. Abrams, Inc., 1971.

Hamilton, Richard. *The Bride Stripped Bare by Her Bachelors, Even.* A typographical version by Richard Hamilton of Duchamp's *Green Box.* Translated by George Heard Hamilton. London: Lund, Humphries and Co. Ltd., 1960.

Henderson, Linda Dalrymple. *The Fourth Dimension and Non-Euclidean Geometry in Modern Art.* Princeton, NJ: Princeton University Press, 1983.

Hockney, David. *David Hockney.* Edited by Nikos Stangos. Introduction by Henry Geldzahler. London: Thames & Hudson, 1976.

Hans Hofmann. Introduction by Sam Hunter and five essays by Hans Hofmann. New York: Harry N. Abrams, Inc., 1963.

Hughes, Robert. *The Shock of the New.* New York: Alfred A. Knopf, Inc., 1980.

Janis, Harriet and Sidney. *Picasso, the Recent Years 1939–1946.* Garden City, NY: Doubleday and Co. Inc., 1946.

Johnson, Ellen H., ed. *American Artists on Art from 1940 to 1980.* New York: Harper & Row, 1982.

Johnson, Ellen H. *Modern Art and the Object.* New York: Harper & Row, 1976.

Lippard, Lucy. *Eva Hesse.* New York: New York University Press, 1976.

van der Marck, Jan. *The Sculpture of George Segal.* New York: Harry N. Abrams, Inc., 1975.

Mitchell, Charles. "'Very like a whale': the spectator's role in modern art." In *Concerning Contemporary Art,* edited by Bernard Smith, pp. 35–88. New York: Oxford University Press, 1974.

Naifeh, Steven. *Gene Davis.* New York: The Arts Publisher, Inc., 1982.

O'Doherty, Brian. *American Masters: The Voice and the Myth.* New York: Random House, 1974.

Paz, Octavio. *Marcel Duchamp: Appearance Stripped Bare.* Translated by Rachel Phillips and Donald Gardner. New York: The Viking Press, 1978.

Peppiatt, Michael and Bellony-Rewald, Alice. *Imagination's Chamber.* Boston: Little, Brown & Co. A New York Graphic Society Book, 1982.

Fairfield Porter: Art in Its Own Terms, Selected Criticism, 1935–75. Edited, with introduction, by Rackstraw Downes. New York: Taplinger, 1979.

Robbins, Daniel. "Cubism and Its Affinities." In *Great Drawings of All Times: The Twentieth-Century,* edited by Victoria Thorson. Redding, CT: Talisman Books, 1979.

Rosenblum, Robert. *Modern Painting and the Northern Romantic Tradition: Friedrich to Rothko.* New York: Harper & Row, 1975.

Scharf, Aaron. *Art and Photography.* New York: Penguin Books, 1968.

Schmoll, J. A. gen Eisenwerth. "Fensterbilder: Motivketten in der europäischen Malerei" in *Beiträge zur Motivkunde des 19. Jahrhunderts,* by Ludwig Grote, pp. 13–165. Munich: Prestel-Verlag, 1970.

Schneider, Pierre. *Matisse.* New York: Rizzoli International Publications, 1984.

Schrade, Hubert. *German Romantic Painting.* Translated by Maria Pelikan. New York: Harry N. Abrams, Inc., 1967.

Stealingworth, Slim. *Tom Wesselmann.* New York: Abbeville Press, 1980.

Steinberg, Leo. *Other Criteria: Confrontations with Twentieth-Century Art.* New York: Oxford University Press, 1972.

Sylvester, David. *Magritte.* New York: Praeger, 1969.

Vriesen, Gustav and Imdahl, Max. *Robert Delaunay: Light and Color.* New York: Harry N. Abrams, Inc., 1967.

Waldman, Diane. *Joseph Cornell.* New York: George Braziller, Inc., 1977.

————. *Ellsworth Kelly: Drawings, Collages, Prints.* Greenwich, CT: New York Graphic Society, 1971.

Werner, Alfred. *Raoul Dufy.* New York: Harry N. Abrams, Inc., 1971.

Exhibition Catalogues

After Matisse. Essays by Tiffany Bell, Dore Ashton and Irving Sandler. New York: Independent Curators Incorporated, 1986.

Siah Armajani: bridges, houses, communal spaces, dictionary for building. Essays by Janet Kardon and Kate Linker. Philadelphia, PA: Institute of Contemporary Art, University of Pennsylvania, 1985.

Art about Art. Text by Jean Lipman and Richard Marshall. Introduction by Leo Steinberg. New York: E. P. Dutton with Whitney Museum of American Art, 1978.

Richard Artschwager's Theme(s). Essays by Richard Armstrong, Linda Cathcart, and Suzanne Delehanty. Buffalo, NY: Albright–Knox Art Gallery; Philadelphia, PA: Institute of Contemporary Art; and La Jolla, CA: La Jolla Museum of Contemporary Art, 1979.

Balthus. Text by Sabine Rewald. New York: Harry N. Abrams, Inc., with The Metropolitan Museum of Art, 1984.

Chagall. Text by Susan Compton. London: Weidenfeld and Nicholson with Royal Academy of Arts, 1985.

Joseph Cornell. Edited by Kynaston McShine. Essays by Dawn Ades, Carter Ratcliff, P. Adams Sitney, Lynda Roscoe Hartigan. New York: The Museum of Modern Art, 1980.

D'un Espace à l'Autre: La Fenêtre. Oeuvres du XXᵉ siècle. Essays by Alain Mousseigne and others. Nice, France: Musée de l'Annonciade, 1978.

Richard Diebenkorn: Paintings and Drawings, 1943–1980. Revised edition with essays by Robert T. Buck, Jr., Linda Cathcart, Gerald Nordland, Maurice Tuchman. New York: Rizzoli International Publications with Albright–Knox Art Gallery, 1980.

Marcel Duchamp. Edited by Anne d'Harnoncourt and Kynaston McShine. New York: The Museum of Modern Art and Philadelphia, PA: Philadelphia Museum of Art, 1973.

Einblicke–Ausblicke: Fensterbilder von der Romantik bis heute. Essay by J. A. Schmoll gen. Eisenwerth. Recklinghausen, Germany: Städtische Kunsthalle Recklinghausen, 1976.

Richard Estes: The Urban Landscape. Essay by John Canaday. Catalogue and interview by John Arthur. Boston, MA: New York Graphic Society with Museum of Fine Arts, 1978.

Adolph Gottlieb: A Retrospective. Text by Lawrence Alloway and Mary Davis MacNaughton. New York: The Arts Publisher, Inc., with Adolph and Esther Gottlieb Foundation, 1981.

Adolph Gottlieb Paintings 1921–1956. Introduction by Miriam Roberts. Omaha, NB: Joslyn Art Museum, 1979.

Juan Gris. Text by Mark Rosenthal. New York: Abbeville Press with University Art Museum, University of California, Berkeley, 1983.

Juan Gris. Edited by Gary Tinterow. Essay by Mark Rosenthal. Madrid: Ministerio de cultura, 1985.

Marsden Hartley. Text by Barbara Haskell. New York: New York University Press with Whitney Museum of American Art, 1980.

Eva Hesse: A Retrospective of the Drawings. Text by Ellen H. Johnson. Oberlin, OH: Allen Memorial Art Museum, Oberlin College, 1982.

Howard Hodgkin. Introduction by Richard Morphet. London: The Tate Gallery, 1985.

Edward Hopper: The Art and the Artist. Text by Gail Levin. New York: W. W. Norton with Whitney Museum of American Art, 1980.

Neil Jenney: Paintings and Sculpture 1967–1980. Text by Mark Rosenthal. Statements by Neil Jenney. Berkeley, CA: University Art Museum, University of California, n.d.

Jasper Johns. Text by Michael Crichton. New York: Harry N. Abrams, Inc., with Whitney Museum of American Art, 1977.

Ellsworth Kelly. Text by E. G. Goosen. New York: The Museum of Modern Art, 1973.

Edward and Nancy Reddin Kienholz: Human Scale. Essays by Laurence Wescher, Edward Kienholz, and Ron Glowen. San Francisco, CA: San Francisco Museum of Modern Art, 1984.

Roy Lichtenstein. Text by Jack Cowart. New York: Hudson Hills Press, Inc., with the Saint Louis Art Museum, 1981.

Sylvia Plimack Mangold: Paintings 1965–1982. Introduction by Thomas H. Garver. Madison, WI: Madison Art Center, 1983.

Robert Moskowitz. Essay by Katy Kline. New York: Blum Helman Gallery, 1986.

Robert Motherwell. Essays by Dore Ashton and Jack D. Flam with an introduction by Robert T. Buck. New York: Abbeville Press with Albright–Knox Art Gallery, 1983.

Catherine Murphy. Essay by Linda Nochlin. New York: Xavier Fourcade, Inc., 1985.

New Image Painting. Essay by Richard Marshall. New York: Whitney Museum of American Art, 1978.

Mark Rothko, 1903–1970: A Retrospective. Text by Diane Waldman. New York: Harry N. Abrams, Inc., with The Solomon R. Guggenheim Foundation, 1978.

Edouard Vuillard 1868–1940. Foreword by Mario Amaya. Essays by John Russell and others. London: Thames & Hudson with Art Gallery of Ontario, Canada, 1971.

John Walker. Essay by Jack Flam. Washington, DC: The Phillips Collection, 1982.

Wiley Territory. Essays by Graham W. J. Beal and John Perreault. Minneapolis, MN: Walker Art Center, 1979.

Window Room Furniture. Introduction by Tod Williams and Ricardo Scofidio. New York: Rizzoli International Publications with The Cooper Union, 1981.

Periodicals

Adams, Brooks. "Zen and the Art of Video." *Art in America* (February 1984): 123–26.

Arnason, H. H. "The Wall and the Window." *Art News* (Summer 1969): 48–52.

Baker, Amy. Interview with Ralph Humphrey, "Painterly Edge." *Artforum* (April 1982): 38–43.

Baker, Kenneth. "Material Feelings." *Art in America* (October 1984): 162–67.

Buckberrough, Sherry A. "The Simultaneous Content of Robert Delaunay's Windows." *Arts Magazine* (September 1979): 102–11.

Eitner, Lorenz. "The Open Window and the Storm Tossed Boat." *Art Bulletin* (December 1955): 281–90.

Gottlieb, Carla. "The Role of the Window in the Art of Matisse." *The Journal of Aesthetics and Art Criticism* (Summer 1964): 393–423.

Henry, Gerrit. "Gene Davis: Window Paintings." *Arts Magazine* (April 1978): 154–55.

———. "Jane Freilicher and the Real Thing." *Art News* (January 1985): 78–83.

Higgins, Judith. "In a Hot Country." *Art News* (Summer 1985): 56–65.

Kuspit, Donald B. "Delaunay's rationale for *Peinture Pure,* 1909–1912." *Art Journal* (Winter 1974–75): 108–14.

Levine, Steven Z. "The Window Metaphor and Monet's Windows." *Arts Magazine* (November 1979): 98–104.

Neff, John Hallmark. "Painting and Perception: Don Eddy." *Arts Magazine* (December 1979): 98–102.

Rouve, Pierre. "Open Window." *Art News and Review* (February 15, 1958): 5.

Silberman, Robert. "Imitation of Life." *Art in America* (March 1986): 138–43.

Stuckey, Charles F. "Duchamp's Acephalic Symbolism." *Art in America* (January 1979): 94–99.

NEUBERGER MUSEUM STAFF

Wilfred Arevalo, Maintenance Head
Jeanette Blackburn, Guard
Eleanor Phillips Brackbill, Head of Museum Education
Douglas Caulk, Museum Manager
Meryl Cohen, Registrar
Kevin Concannon, Coordinator of Public Programs
John Conway, Preparator*
Olga D'Angelo, Curatorial Assistant
John Davis, Exhibitions Coordinator
Suzanne Delehanty, Director
Judith Dykema, Public Information Consultant*
Carol Engler, Assistant to the Museum Manager
Susanne Fateh-Tehrani, Preparator*
Karen Gausch, Preparator*
Sigrid Goldiner, Research Assistant*
Jewel Hoogstoel, Development Assistant
Patricia Magnani, Assistant Registrar*
Victoria Malits, Education Secretary
Nancy Miller, Assistant Director
Susan Mroczynski, Membership Secretary
Jeff Nash, Preparator*
Karen G. Nelson, Coordinator of Educational Services
Anne Ocone, NEA Apprentice
Claire Powers, Administrative Assistant
Michael Prudhom, Preparator*
Michael Reed, Special Project Consultant*
Edmonde Reusch, Head Guard
Maria Ritacco, Maintenance
Jane Steinberg, Bookshop Manager*
Timothy Tranzillo, Preparator*
Randy Williamson, Guard
*Part-time

PHOTOGRAPHY CREDITS

Photographers are listed alphabetically. Credits are supplied by page number. Where no photographic credit is given, the photograph has been graciously provided by the owner or the lender.

Yura Adams Photography (page 54)
Jörg P. Anders (illus. 4, 10)
Nicolo Orsi Battaglini (illus. 2)
Larry Bercow (page 31)
Rudolph Burckhardt (pages 82 bottom, 93)
Michael Cavanagh and Kevin Montague (back cover and illus. 16)
Geoffrey Clements (pages 88, 96)
Bevan Davies (page 44)
eeva-inkeri (page 64 top)
Ali Elai (page 67)
Roy M. Elkind (page 94)
John A. Ferrari (pages 60 bottom, 61 top)
Jim Frank (pages 76, 97 bottom)
Gamma One Conversions (page 37)
Hickey and Robertson, courtesy Menil Foundation (page 70)
Brad Iverson (page 95)
Bill Jacobson (pages 78, 79)
Bruce B. Jones (page 82 top)
Zini Lardieri (page 59 bottom)
Martinelli Photography (page 36)
Wayne McCall (page 89)
Richard P. Meyer (page 48)
Andrew Moore (page 98)
Peter Moore (page 55)
Otto E. Nelson (page 4)
Harvey Osterhoudt and Ken Strothman (page 69)
Philadelphia Museum of Art (page 56, illus. 15)
Eric Pollitzer (pages 45 top, 45 right, 47, 53, 103)
Pollitzer, Strong and Meyer (pages 33, 35, 92)
Quesada/Burke (page 97 top)
Earl Ripling (page 61 bottom)
Kevin Ryan (page 87 top and bottom)
E.G. Schemf (page 64 bottom)
John D. Schiff (illus. 15)
Steven Sloman (pages 41, 42)
Ivan Dalla Tana (pages 38, 7)
Thomas P. Vinetz (page 51)
Wolfgang Volz (page 91)
Dorothy Zeidman (page 66)
Alan Zindman (page 60 top)

Aren't you our geometry
window, very simple shape
circumscribing our enormous
life painlessly?

A lover's never so beautiful
as when we see her appear
framed by you; because, window,
you make her most immortal.

All risks are cancelled. Being
stands at love's center,
with this narrow space around,
where we are master.

RAINER MARIA RILKE
"Windows III" 1926

For G.B.D.